Prologue

Daddy's Run

"Boo! Come quick!"
yelled a voice in the night
"Boo! Can't you hear me?"
My heart filled with fright.
I can't tell you the thoughts
that raced through my mind
when my dad yelled for me,
it was different this time.
"Boy, run for the doctor!"
was all that dad said

I barely heard
his voice faint in my head.
I looked round the room
(that I'd rarely been in)
The things that I saw
made my head more than spin
There were two huge shadows,
one human, one blob)
As I stood in the doorway
my stomach tied in knots
Old gray buckets from the well
sat on the floor
Filled with steaming water,
I didn't want to see more
A voice deep inside said,
"You have to look."
I forced my eyes open
and oh the look that I took
Dad had an old, tattered cloth
he was wringing in his hands
The blood that dripped from it
made me understand
That my childhood had left me
when I stepped inside

My parents' bedroom
on that warm summer night
Mama, my mama
was soaked in her sweat
Her body shivered silently
as she lay on their bed
Pulled way up,
her gown rested high on her thighs
Then, she saw me,
I looked in her eyes
Her mouth opened slowly
I heard her lips part
No other sound in the room
'cept the beating of my heart
Her head turned away
something came over me
Crawled over my body
from my head to my feet
First it was warmth
that flowed down my back
That warm cuddly feeling
like after a bath
It caressed my body
went through to my soul
Quickly it was gone
I felt ice cold

"Boy! Run for the doctor!"
my daddy cried
I didn't like what I saw
when I looked into his eyes
Something was not right
his eyes full of fear?
On the brim of his eyelids
I thought I saw tears
"Boo! Go now!"
was the last thing I heard

As I turned to leave
without uttering a word
With all that had happened
only seconds had passed
My feet glided quickly
over brown spotty grass
My feet are so tired,
Lord knows I can't stop
"There it is! I can see it!
There's the doctor's house!
Thank you Jesus! I made it!
Whew! Thank you Lord!"
But I,
I can't just knock
on a white man's door
Daddy told me never,
mama told me too
I'm cold and scared,
don't know what to do?
Boo wrestled with himself
till his hand touched the door
Knocked gently, then harder as he prayed
"Help me Lord!"
The doctor grabbed his bag, no pause in his step
Together in the dark they made their way back
Just in time to see a sheet pulled over mama's head
Boo sank to the floor
his mom was dead
That boy grew up to be a daddy
matured into a man
who spent his whole life wondering
trying to understand
If his hesitation cost his mama her life
That man was my father
Annie Mae was his wife

HESITATIONS

Cover design by Dominique Renée

ISBN 978-1-66785-172-3

This book is dedicated to:
my daughter Dominique and my son Kyle,
for believing in dreams and having the courage
to pursue them. You continue to inspire me.
I want to be just like you when I grow up!

Special thanks to: Adam Campbell, Beverly Cobbs,
Barbara Dalio, Renee Graham, Ricky Graham,
Toya Graham, Cyndy Heard, Agnes Joines, Betty Moore,
Bernice Seward, Shaun Smith and Doris Thurman
Your words of encouragement,
mixed with keeping it real,
(you know who you are ☺,)
finally pushed me past my hesitation.

In memory of:
My parents-Annie and Freddie Graham,
Siblings-Fredrecia Graham Spinola and Vinny Graham
You are loved and missed...
and
Casey Thurman
Thanks for teaching me what worship really means
(and for sharing your mom with me.)

CONTENTS

HESITANT
TO TRUST

Cokoa, our cat, was absolutely gorgeous but she had serious trust issues. She didn't take to a lot of people but loved my children, blankets, and me. Pebbles, a homeless kitten, was able to win her over and get accepted into our small circle. It was nothing for Cokoa to cozy up to someone and then within minutes strike at them as if she had never met them before. If she didn't like you at all, that was made crystal clear. I prayed for our veterinarian every time she was due for a checkup.

Cokoa and I had more in common than I would like to admit. Trust, or lack of, in God and people, has been a challenge for me. I was raised in a household where church attendance was not optional. Anything you were asked to do as part of a worship service or Sunday school, only had one response available, yes. Even the tone of that yes had to meet a certain standard. As I grew into adulthood my trust in God and people consistently wavered. I thought church members were supposed to be perfect and when I found that was not the case, I began to doubt everything I had ever been taught. As a result, my relationships with God and people suffered. Pieces in this section reflect that. They are not in any special order because on any given day they may represent my current state of mind. I am a work in progress.

I Sit

I sit
as if
it was a Monday
Exhausted
but excited
at the same time
Tired of the endless searching
for reality
Excited about ideas that race
through my mind
about
the future
my dreams
my desires
my goals
that steep
deep inside
fueled by my soul
that
refuses to die
despite
the forces
that fight
to infest my spirit
and bid me
goodnight
I sit
as if
I'm still trapped inside
the child
that struggled
afraid to cry
or admit
that her tears
her dreams

and her fears
were real
admit she could feel
the eyes that stared
the comments that blared
her secrets being shared
while she never dared
to speak
a word
that wouldn't have been heard
But now
I WON'T sit
as if
I've forgotten whose I am
Sometimes defeated
but
still victorious
'cause
My God has a plan
That will lift me from all that is holding me back
strengthen my faith
mount an attack
on
anything
and everything
One by one
till it's done
and
I REMAIN STANDING
'cause my battle's been won
A writer
a speaker
and biblically true to my parents
my ancestors
my God
through and through

Choosing To Die

Choosing to die
As I cry
Wondering why it has to be this way
Why I ask as I think of the past
Wishing it would last long enough to change your mind
and change the pain I feel
As my mind reels
tries to deal
With what is happening now
What is taking place (what I want to erase)
what I have to face
'Cause it's not moving at my pace
If you proceed (as you've led us to believe) you will
I have to be still
I must respect your choice of death and really rest
In the arms of my father (the one I claim to cling to)
As I realize, how much I love you
I truly do
Your choice, (as my tears stand poised)
Must be the focus of my prayers
Your right to die
Dignified
Your peace
As you leave to be with Jesus
Who will help me to see
This is not about me
You choosing to die
Is making me cry
As I wonder why
But know I can't deny
Your choice
To die
Dignified
Goodbye

I love Jesus But

I love Jesus but
I still have days when I feel weary
Days when I'm downright tired
Days when I feel quite lonely
Days when I want to be fired
From
everything
my job,
my family,
my commitments,
my life!
Because
on the days when my mind is weary
days when my energy is spent
days when my heart is lonely
and my body feels broken
and bent
into positions
uncomfortable positions
painful positions,
that I cannot control
In the midst of my suffering
I hear a voice
echo through my soul
"I STILL WANT YOU!
So, you must
stand firm my daughter,
stand firm like my son
Your work is not over,
no, your work is not done"
...God has given us eternal life
and this life is in His son (1 John 5:11)
He gives strength to the weary
and increases the power of the weak (Isaiah 40:29)
They will still bear fruit in old age

he says they will stay fresh and green (Psalm 92:14)
Is there a promise God made
that He wouldn't keep? No
So, you must stand firm my sister
Stand firm my brother
and allow yourself to experience a love like none other
A love no earthly man can give
A love that allows us to breathe, to live
We must stand firm
for the next chapter in our story
That will be written quite clearly
"to my Father's glory,
That you bear much fruit showing yourselves to be
my disciples (John 15:8) avoiding eternity in Hell
...Hold unswervingly
to the hope we profess
For He who promised (Hebrews 10:23)
shows his faithfulness
Your spiritual gift did not get up and leave...
"My God is my rock in whom I take refuge,
He is my shield
And the horn of my salvation my stronghold (Psalm 18:2)
So, for Him
I'll continue to serve and be bold.
Bold as I remember His death at Calvary
Bold as eyes for those who cannot see
Bold as I speak of his love that he shares
Bold as ears for those who cannot hear
Bold as feet for those who cannot walk
Bold as I speak for those who cannot talk
Boldly rejoice, boldly believe,
Boldly give of myself, boldly receive
He still wants me
I know He wants you to
Reach out
Allow Him to show you what to do

I Rock

I rock to calm my heart

I rock to ease my mind

I rock to still my crying

I rock most all the time

I rock when I'm excited

I rock when I'm depressed

I rock when things are going great

I rock when I am stressed

I rock because I'm freezing

I rock because I'm hot

I rock to keep from sleeping

I rock, can't seem to stop

I rock when the Spirit moves me

I rock when my spirit's not right

I rock first thing in the morning

I rock in the deep of the night

I rock because it takes me

back to my momma's arms

I rock 'cause it takes me to a place

where I can't be harmed

I rock because it soothes me

it medicates my soul

I rock because Jesus cradles me

when I rock

Criminal Mind

Criminal mind
of a different kind
But
still a criminal mind
Robbing self of destiny
Allowing thoughts of despair
Choosing not to try
Stuck in my chair
It's a crime
to tell Jesus
I cannot move
I'm in Contempt
Lock me up
I guess that's what I choose
If I remain tied to my criminal mind
stealing what to me doesn't belong
walking around whistling
the same old song
I'm sad, pity me
I can't cause I'm hurt
Nobody loves me
Will help me
I'm in contempt of court
for lying to self
What a waste of time
Refusing the love of Jesus
what a criminal mind
My diagnosis
might read something like this
Contributing factors
we've got on our list

Between 45-55
not too tall or too short
has avoided the system
probably divorced
has children and has hidden
inside of their dreams
now they are their own people
her life is busting at the seams
Can't hide in indecision
truth is calling her name
being pushed into life
this time it's no game
Has a weapon called faith
which she's been forced to use
She keeps adjusting her weapon
She's got nothing to lose
The high she received
when she used it the first time
Is all she can think about
so she's destined to try
to get high again
on the drug of her choice
In the spirit of faith
as she faces the court

Criminal mind
of a different kind
But for Jesus this time

How Far Will We Reach to Share God's Love?

How far will we reach to share God's love?
To those who are hungry and not sitting on pews
but sitting outside storefronts with no soles on their shoes
but a soul reaching out from deep down inside
an appetite and thirst that the world can't satisfy

To those who have needs that are unlike our own
who limp when they walk and often groan,
from the pain that they feel from the pains in their legs
or their hips, their hearts, their arms, and their heads

Do our hands steady their step or speed up their fall
by standing close by but not reaching at all.
to those whom we know and profess to love
when loving involves sacrifice and changes, huh

Will our hands become glued to the lint in our pockets?
Our sight focus only on our eyelids and eye sockets?
How far will we reach? Will arthritis come by?
With her fiancée bursitis and kids paralysis and sty?
In the eyes of our Lord are we reaching His sight?
Or are our fingertips barely touching
his tears shed at night?
Are our fingertips wet from the rim of His tears?
As they float down from heaven
from the heavy heart He bears?
A heart overflowing with distress and hurt from the words that
He said, that are simply not heard
by those of us with our hands held over our ears
who cannot reach out to anyone while we hold them there
to keep out the call to service, the call to submit
the call to study, the call to real worship
the call to a relationship given to you & me
My fellow Christian how far will we reach?

The Pen of my Heart

It is the pen
that balances my heart
keeps it beating
when the devil thinks
he's defeating me.

It is the ink
flowing from the pen
that rescues me again and again
as lucifer shouts
"Don't let her win.
Hit her again
harder, harder!"
But God doesn't barter
for me.
It is the gravity
that eases the ink
from the pen,
that graces my hand
often,
at your command.
I know you understand,
as do I, that it is You
who controls the hand
that holds the pen,
the gravity
that controls the flow of the ink,
where it goes,
every word,
every drop,
when it starts,
and when it stops
thus,
You,
control my heart.

Sometimes

Sometimes
it is overwhelming
emotions raw
exploding
uncontrolled
simply because
I am in Your presence
amongst your people
in awe of those who have suffered
but
stand firm
despite the pity their circumstances could earn them
despite the loss of their loved ones,
their parents
their children
their spouse
their jobs
their health
their titles
their house
surrounded by them
I am in Your presence
They will not be moved
just like a tree that's planted by the water ♪
I too shall not be moved
I am forever Your daughter

Worship (for Casey)

There's a feeling inside
that's hard to describe
When I'm here in worship with you
For I see and feel Jesus
He's in your hugs
your words of love
He's here and He greets me

There's a joy that explodes
deep down in my soul
When I'm here in worship with you
For I feel and taste Jesus
He's in your songs
which serenade me all week long
Jesus is here and He meets me

There's a peace that caresses
invades, and blesses me
When I'm here in worship with you
For I taste, see, and feel Jesus
He's in the word that is preached, the truth that I seek
Jesus reaches out and touches me

But don't misunderstand me
and think that when I leave you
Jesus doesn't leave with me
You see, I worship and praise throughout all my days
Not just when I am with you
There are lives that are changed from the unrestrained
Worship that daily I do

I believe you Casey
There's a glow that you wear
whenever you're here
When you come to worship with us
For in you I see and feel Jesus
In your greetings there's His grace
Jesus' Joy on your face
He is within you, and He greets me
There's a peace that you give
that is truly a gift
When you come to worship with us
For in you is the spirit of Jesus
He's in the peace of your ministry
Through you
He continues to bless me
Continue this walk
continue to love,
and worship our Heavenly Father above
For no eye has seen,
no ear has heard
all that Jesus will do through you,
as you continue to serve

Sisters in Unity

We can't afford to lose the feeling that we now have
This deep unconditional love that cements our paths
together
as we groove towards Christ,
His wisdom
His majesty
His power
His might
His might that leveled mountains of jealousy,
envy and hurt
to reduce us to seedlings... fertilized, giving new birth
to friendships
partnerships
fellowship
and support...
New birth to the reason we breathe
and the reason we were born
Born to worship and serve as sisters in love
With a powerful, heavenly Father who sits high above
and also within
each one of our hearts
We CAN'T lose this feeling though we're now apart
From the place... Where he met us
On a level so deep
We were moved from our pews
to our feet,
to our knees,
to our shouting,
to our wailing,
moved through our pain
and to our praising
that showered us more than the rain
of our tears
The tears that broke us...
taught us to moan,

Flushed away our pride in material homes
and our outward appearance of S. S. A. M. D.
You know Superiority, Seniority and About Me Disease
Our tears melted away
all that crud on the outside
As we laughed
prayed
hugged
even danced
and cried
We can't lose this feeling
but sisters we can share
with our families,
our church,
at work
everywhere
Share our love
our commitment
our vision
our Christ
our Witness
our experience
our testimony
our lives
and
our journey
as we move forth
released & free
in Christ
Free in love
and walking in UNITY

He Is Holy (for Dominique)

Try not to take it personally,
But
This is one time
when it IS All ABOUT ME!!

Because as you seek to judge me
He does something called edify me
The more you seek to control me
my angels are dispatched to counsel and cover me
The more you try to intimidate me
The more He seeks to comfort me
And if you dare try to dominate me
My Father will strengthen me

He is the air I breathe
the wind that carries me
He is Holy

Although I'm stained by sin
He purifies me
He is Holy

He teaches,
convicts
And sanctifies me
He is Holy

Why?
Why... does He do these things?
Because I know I've been created to worship
I know I've been created to serve
I know I'm to give God ALL the glory,
the glory He so rightly deserves
I know its my purpose to bear His fruit
so don't let me confuse you , my swag or my youth

Thinking about attacking me?
Sweetie... don't even start
'cause I've got the seal of Jesus,
covering my heart

He is my sword and my shield
He is Holy

He's my wheel in the middle of a wheel
He is Holy

He's my healer , my deliverer
He is Holy

He's my strong tower
He is Holy

Alpha and Omega
He is Holy

The Ruler of all Rulers
He is Holy

My offense and my defense
He is Holy

My best friend
He is Holy

I will never be the same
He is Holy
and
Holy is His name...

The CREATION vs. CREATOR

(a response to James Weldon Johnson's The Creation)
And man stepped away from his place
And he looked around and said
I'm not satisfied-
I'll make me my own world

And as far as the eye could see
Man desired more things
Bigger and brighter than a diamond in
moonlight
And in these things, he placed his pride
Man smiled, as the devil spoke,
And thoughts of greed rolled up on one side,
While envy stood spying on the other,
And man said, "This is good!"

Man reached out and took even more matters
into his own defiled hands,
Abandoning the commandments
God had given to man
Until... he felt he was done
And he sat among –
His things gathered up in his home
Where he was never alone,
'cause having things birthed theft,
deceit and new darkness,
Which required more light to keep away the
night
But... man valued this world;
Man said, "This is Good!"

Man stepped out on the solid ground
beneath his feet
Enjoying the sun, the moon and the stars drifting
silently above his head,
and said

I control it all... and stood even more tall
As he trod toward the valleys of wickedness,
licentiousness and slander
(raising God's dander)

But there he stopped, looked and saw
That his world had lost some of its beauty.
So he stepped further over the edge
into the folly of adultery
and not even the words of Moses flashing in
his mind helped at this time...

"Neither add to nor take away from,
the commandments of the LORD
To show wisdom and discernment
they must be diligently observed
To God, man spat words from his lips
that never touched the tip
of his heart
Murder became art,
He batted his eyes everywhere but within
And applauded his own achievements;
Even as the waters of the earth dwindled down,
Till less and less could be found.
And new dangers sprouted,
And battles blossomed, (As man played possum)
and pointed his finger to the sky,
Yelling why???

God spread out his arms,
And this time man wasn't harmed
And the rivers ran once more down to the sea;
And man smiled again, quite pleased
and said, "This is good!"
And as sunshine reappeared,
Dancing daintily around his ears
And curled itself around his shoulder.

Man raised his arm and got even bolder
And sighed
"I'm in charge again"
And quicker than man could drop his hand.
Disaster covered all the land
Fish, fowls, beasts, birds, and man
became diseased
Poisoned and contaminated like the rivers
and the seas,

Stunned... man hobbled around,
And looked around
On all that had made him glad
The fortress he lived in
all that he had.
Material things still glistening,
Like the problems they caused
And then man finally,
Willfully thought,
"Why am I not satisfied still."

Then Man fell down on his knees
On the side of a road where there used to be trees
So he could think;
On his sore, swollen knees he fell down;
With his head on his hands,
Man thought as he frowned,
Of all he created that now stood in the way
Of the God
The Creator and all He had to say
Man thought Of the Lord of all power
The Lord of all might,
the author of the world
and giver of all true light:
By the side of the road
on his sore swollen knees

with his head on his hands
man cried out and said,
"Please Dear God, forgive me
Forgive me my sins"
As he curled into fetal comfort
He whispered.
"Let me be born again."

Up from his world of affliction
God scooped up this man;
And in the crystal-clear river
He blessed Him again;
And the great God Almighty
Who chose a tapestry of gold for the sun
and placed it in a patient blue sky,
Who scattered the bright delicate stars
to their homes in the night,
Who shaped the earth in the center
of His smooth firm hands;
This Great God,
Like a mother
bending over her baby for the first time,
Kneeled down in the dust
rejoicing over the lump of clay
He had shaped in His own image.
that returned to Him this day
And then into him
He blew the breath of fresh life,
and man became born again.
Amen.
Amen.

I'm Totally His

I missed maybe six,
seven years of my life
in a self-induced coma
Injured, barely breathing
brain not really functioning
Life support the only thing keeping me going,
one line
the mainline
Injured by society
literally crushed by man
Couldn't seem to rebound
Couldn't understand
So, I got busy for Jesus
(I thought)
In a fog
I worked sometimes 15 hours a day
Doing good for others
The life support
made me function
Kept my heart going
so my organs continued to work
While injured
hurt deeply
too deep to discuss
too painful to remember
So
I got more busy
Sometimes 20 hours a day
Serving anyone and everyone
because Jesus would want it that way
I thought
But did He? Does He
want that for my life?
Is that why He saved me
and put me aside

To live through doing for others
and deny self
I realized, hopefully not too late
there's something else
Jesus wants me
to grow in him
to talk to him
to walk with him
hand in hand
To allow him inside of me
to soak me within
with his love not just for others
but his love for me
and that was the part that I just didn't see
While I ran nonstop for 6 maybe 7 years
I neglected my body
I neglected my tears
I ignored my pain
I ignored my sight
no mirrors around me
so everything could be right
I've been taken off life support
I'll either swim or drown
The first few moments I spent floundering around
I was used to life
as it was, didn't want change
It's so much easier to leave things the same
While I run around helping
I don't feel my feet
crying for mercy or maybe just a seat
While I run around being helpful
I can't see I need
a godly man walking beside me
While I run around with help as my middle name
I can't hear my body
crying for change
Can't feel, can't see, can't hear

Can't even bleed
Till I stop
and stand still
life support gone
and see for the first time
what's really going on
I thought I was serving Jesus
but I've been in his way
preventing the growth of others
ignorant of my faith
By rushing to meet every need that they have
I don't have time to see anything
no time to be sad
They don't need Jesus 'cause they've got me
Why would they ever get down on their knees?
Get down on the ground
and dirty their pants
(Which I would have taken to the cleaners
if they gave me a chance)
Why do anything for themselves
like grow in the Lord?
'Cause I'll take care of everything
that's what I was for
Now
I love my sisters
and I love my brothers
but I love my Jesus and myself before others
I need to have time
to sit so I can grow
I need to face the mirror
to finally know
what I look like
Is it his image I project?
Do I love the Lord Truly?
Am I showing respect?
On in some respect
Have I undermined his power?

Usurped his authority
darn near devoured
the needs of others
while sacrificing my own
A martyr for what?
I don't even know
The mirror is calling
new injuries
new pain
as I look at all
that I know I must change
As I see the damage
the tears start to flow
I didn't know seeing myself could hurt so
I sink down to a heap in the floor
I submit
my life to you Lord
Something I thought I'd done before
The tears won't stop
what else do you want?
What else is it Jesus that I could have done?
Reveal to me Jesus
make it crystal clear
Cause I just don't see
glasses fogged up with tears
"Take them off," a voice said
"Take them off and see me"
I cried for so long that it hurt
I was sick.
Been sick for longer than I knew
Sicker than those I was helping
But Jesus knew
Breathing was difficult, coughing was quick
I ran to grab tissues. I started to spit
Up and out
Spirits, that can't live within
If I want Jesus then they've got to go

I need all the room I can get for Him
I coughed up confusion
and low self esteem
I coughed up distress
and hindrances to my dreams
I coughed up busyness
and refusing to stand still
I coughed up obstacles to doing God's will
I coughed up the doubts that I could really be blessed
I coughed and coughed till there was nothing left
but Jesus and me
A Saved sinner
All is not lost
"Don't you know I died for you?
upon a cross"
Forgive me was all that came to my mind
Forgive me I said
So many times
Forgive me Lord Jesus
For all the wrongs that I've done
Seen and unseen
For not trusting before serving
Simply for not being
a good steward of my body,
a good steward of my life
a good steward of my soul
a good steward of my time
my mind, my finances
and to all that I have been blind
Forgive me Lord Jesus
Please wash me clean
The crying has stopped
I'm dealing with what I've seen
But that's okay
'cause I've learned from what I missed
I've been reborn and I'm totally his

Vinny

He was born prematurely, but born right on time
Died prematurely circled through my mind
As I tried to make sense of a life cut so short
A life you allowed God you permit to be born
"God didn't you hear me?
Were you listening as I prayed
for you to fix him, to heal him, to let him stay?"
"I heard you and I answered you," came the reply
In my anger my response was, "answer denied"
In my anger I thought, didn't you see how he served?
He suffered in silence never mumbled a word
though pain perforated his body
he worked on; didn't you see?
He served to your glory even the least of these
From baby squirrels, to kittens, puppies, or ants
he didn't want anything to die not even a plant
So, God why? "Did you hear what I said?"
"I heard you and answered you, that's why he's not dead.
I blessed him with twenty-one extra years"
Thinking about that slowed the flow of my tears
"He still had his sight and all his limbs
He still had his pride and carried me within
He prayed to me steadily and sought out my will
His life had a purpose, the purpose was fulfilled!"
Tears flowed freely as I sat, thought for awhile
Till my tears dribbled down to the creases in my smile
Where they fit quite comfortably soothing my soul
My anger grew distant, from hot to cold
"I asked you to prolong his life, you did
His life expectancy 23, to 44 he lived"
"You had him longer than I had my own son
His battle is over, his victory is won
And now he resides here rejoicing with me
Forever free from his pain here in eternity!"

I Prayed

Last night,
I prayed for you
That somewhere way down deep inside
You'll find the strength that you will need
To put up with the likes of me
I prayed for you.

I prayed for me
That way down deep within my soul
Patience and unselfish ways will grow
and thus, the seeds of love we'll sow
I prayed for me.

Our children too
that day to day as time goes by
We'll cast our childish ways aside
And be adults for them display our pride
And not let outside forces, force our love to die
I prayed for them

For if our love and faith in God is strong
Together is where we will belong
Standing together for all to see
The blessings we share as a family
And I know in God we'll trust
Because you see
I prayed for us.

Maturing In His Word

Lord I need your direction
As I sit here reflectin'
feeling completely overwhelmed
With emotion (I guess some can tell)
Family, friends, responsibility
Feels as though I've been put on the spot...
Sitting in the hot seat, ready to meet
Who and what might come
as people stare and wonder
which direction I'll fall in next
I know it's a test
'Cause as my father lays prostrate
in his grave
feeling he couldn't save me from the world
being hurled in my direction
I didn't know how deep his love flowed for me,
his dollbaby
Minus a few strands of hair, but kept in prayer
cloth he made with his hands
I didn't know, didn't understand
Or I couldn't hear
Today
my mom may not know me
as I stand before her
I'm not sure she can see,
her eyes spy me
Curiously... wondering maybe
how I got over the hurdles (minus the girdle)
I was forced to wear since the 4th grade
when they thought it would save
me from harm (which instead it caused)
As it attempted to solve the extra weight I carried
while I tarried towards the future
Feeling futile
I smiled

Rather than cry
Would have been inappropriate anyway
as a lady of faith
(which I was supposed to portray
at all times)
'cause Jesus was, is mine
All the time
And we know
GOD IS GOOD ALL THE TIME
And
ALL THE TIME, GOD IS GOOD
'cause he said he would ... be
Even when my husband's family
I say, somewhat casually
Evaded me
Maybe they're embarrassed or ashamed
By the weight that I've gained
FAT made me change
from the inside out
Thank You Lord I shout and prance
Darn near dance
For joy
As my boy
Leans in to see
What I might be
Doing
I don't care
No secrets here
Family
MIA due to disease
Mentally
Physically
Some even spiritually
If you don't mind me being frank
Maybe down right stank
About it

Those who allowed the devil to mustard their eggs
As they try to stand on legs
Wobblin
But not topplin'
Me
Weebles wobble
but they don't' fall down...
and stay!
Yes, I fall down but I get up
Cause
I know the plan that God has for me
Finally
And if you're not strong
Strong enough to step up to where you belong
Then so long
Cause I've got to move on
And if you don't know
where you're supposed to go
On the wrong day I might just tell you so
Don't stay in my path
Cause I will soar on past
As I move forward
In the WORD
I've been given
And you stand there trippin'
Talking junk
That's supposed to stunt
My growth
I DON'T THINK SO!
For I know the plans I have for you declared the LORD
Plans to give you hope and a future!
Ah I thank God I'm maturing in his word!

Divine Appointment

It is in the blessed quietness that I sit
straining to hear your voice
I'm fully aware that my being here was not by choice
You set aside this moment, this date, and this time
to share the next part of this purposeful journey of mine
but to move forward I must face the past
face the pain that dealt a blow to our relationship
caused it
to change

I was on fire for you Jesus
both inside and out
too hot to be handled with no room for doubt
The world couldn't touch me
couldn't make me give in
I was glowing for you Jesus
even the harsh winds
couldn't make me stumble (I thought)
as I stood tall
It could huff and puff but wouldn't make me fall
Without warning
my flames began to flicker
sometimes reduced to sparks
I buried myself in service
I relied on the love in my heart
for your people, the church body
you Jesus, and your word
If I could just get enough in me (I thought)
Your voice would be heard
But my flames fluttered in and out
reduced to smoke, fumes, until sometimes
I couldn't even feel you in the room

Now I realize
You couldn't fit
My service
me, myself, and I were it
My pain
My concerns
My troubles
My trials
lived close to the surface
behind my smile
which, just like my flames
flickered in and out
in when surrounded by others
out when no one's about
That's when I shed my tears, groaned,
and wailed out loud
afraid of the journey,
the past,
what might come out

Would it shadow my service,
bring shame to the throne?
Would your love and the love of others
leave me standing alone?
I need you, desire you and wish to repent
Please forgive me and thank you for time well spent
I vow to move forward one step at a time
Fully aware of your forgiveness
and this divine appointment of time

Chosen

I know today that I'm not just a woman of God
that is not my sole aim
I am God's chosen woman, my path has changed
Looking fine, hair done and wearing fancy clothes
has long been a thing of the past for that's not why He
chose me
me in my brokenness
me in my tears
me searching for love so unaware
of how choices I made were being heavenly sewn
into a fabric no other person has worn
and unlike the clothes that I buy it a perfect fit
I'm not just of woman of God
that's not it
I am God's woman, and He is my man
the only man that's held my hand more than once
Married twice yet that's true
I've heard the third time is the charm
so I'm saying Jesus, I do
I will nurture, teach, share, and give
be responsible, obedient, and remember to live
in your love and wisdom
continue to serve, worship, and learn
while valuing our relationship and committing to my vow
I'm not just a woman of God
but God's chosen woman now

HESITANT
TO BREATHE

On a windy October day, a colleague and I were building a balloon arch for our high school football team to run through. It was homecoming weekend, and we were excited! I loved community building events and this was one of my favorites. Early in the process my colleague asked me if I felt alright. I said yes, we kept on working. She asked a second time. I was getting a little irritated but simply said "yes." The third time she suggested I go into the restroom and check myself. I knew something had to be wrong. When I saw my reflection in the mirror, I was stunned. My face was swollen. My eyes looked like little slits! I hadn't felt a thing, but it was clear something was very wrong.

At the age of forty I was diagnosed with a Natural Rubber Latex allergy. I had never been allergic to anything before. It turned my world upside down. I was told the four surgeries I had, two c-sections and two fibroid tumor removals, (in a ten-year span of time;) was most likely the source. It coincided with the aids epidemic and the switch to latex gloves for surgeries. I never knew how many things were made of latex. At the time of my diagnosis there were more than forty thousand everyday items! It was in things like stethoscopes atm buttons rubber bands, the pieces that balanced my glasses on my nose, the elastic in underclothing and socks, the action figures my son played with, remote control buttons, bathmats, pencil erasers, rubber grip pens, the list... endless. The number of situations I found myself in where there was a lack of understanding regarding this allergy, also endless.

I spent a lot of time fearing death until one day I realized, I was so afraid of dying, that I had stopped living! I had to learn how to breathe, confidently again. These pieces represent that struggle.

Breathe

I know you are speaking to me
I will hold on
moving forward to the destiny
you have for me
Breathe
breathe again
slowly
intentionally
peacefully
feeling you gently reassuring me
"It is well, it is well with my soul ♪"
words more valuable
than all the gold
this world might hold
breathe
feel
I feel your presence
filling me
slowly
intentionally
peacefully
moving me
spiritually
closer to where I am meant to be
gracefully
"I want Jesus, to walk with me ♪"
echoes faintly within me
I'm remembering
where
when

and how
those words
were first introduced to me
passively
floating
melodically
over the flow of the water
mixed hot with cold
cleansing
both the dishes she washed
and the soul
of mama herself
and anyone else
within earshot
got the word

Slowly
passively
freely
"Touch, touch me Lord Jesus ♪"
Speak

I'm listening
intentionally
peacefully
waiting

breathe

Life Is a Trip

Life is a trip (and then some)
Flashback to a dream I had many years ago
Balloons of every color
big balloons
hanging in every room
Me breathing deep
Inhaling everything that I possibly could
and then
moving on to the next room
breathing in again
Deliberately breathing
Consequences in sight,
Deliberately turning my day into night
But I woke up
made some changes
started out fresh
feeling quite good
feeling quite blessed
an invitation to fellowship
with family and friends
time to rejoice
time to make amends
innocently enter
innocently die
while breathing rather strenuously
and wondering why
"I forgot" "I'm sorry" doesn't sound right
as my eyes close for eternity
some refer to as night
goodbye

Going

Going

going home

going

gone

one final moment

one last song

time to remember

time to forget

no need to worry

wonder or fret

going home

going

gone

to the place

I am told I belong

Going home

You're Killing Me

I want to live
but you're killin' me
Every time you float balloons from the cars in your lot
hang them outside of your business
(so others come see what you've got)
tie them to signs as directions to your celebration
host a party with latex balloons as your decoration
Whether it's a birthday,
gospel fest
anniversary,
or graduation
You're killin' me

You're kiddin' me
You who created me
don't know how to fix me?
I realize the fact that you saved me,
surgery after surgery
and through your use of latex gloves
unintentionally
started killin' me
And now, you've got no answers?
You've got to be kiddin' me
You say things like
"What is latex gonna do
jump up and grab you?"
or "We're latex free" and then
proceed to hand me
a rubber grip pen
place me near a row of rubber wheeled wheelchairs
that has no end

And smile all the while as if you're my friend
As I struggle to breathe
You're insulting me
And poisoning me
As you feed me
Restaurant after restaurant
still in the dark ages
Don't know a thing about latex allergies and its stages
You cook for me without thinking
I eat and start drinking
and quickly realize
as the swelling starts round my eyes,
you're poisoning me
without warning
No signs posted saying,
"Latex is used here"
You catch me,
unaware
Yes, you're poisoning me
when you coat newspapers with latex
so no ink gets on your hands
I struggle desperately
to understand
and breathe
while
you're killing me

Tragedy

Tragedy should not have to introduce us to strategy
but all too often she does
doesn't she?
9-ll
Katrina
need I say more?
There stands tragedy
holding the door
and if it's not too late
Strategy, comes in
sometimes so quickly your head will spin
Till you don't know anymore which way is up
This time will she slink in with grace
or trip on some stuff
Will she enter too quickly, too slowly or too late
to win the battle, defeat the crisis we face
Will she pass over the threshold
or simply glance in
and decide to retreat
from what she can't win
as she listens to the murmurs
that I too have heard

"Why should I change what **I'm** doing
to save her?"

"Why would anyone expect me to change?
I might know her by face,
don't know her by name."

"Change for one person,

good gracious, what's next?
Maybe it's time for her to quit,
start a new chapter, new text."
I'm your sister, your mother,
your cousin, your friend
your aunt, significant other,
the one you depend on when tragedy strikes

I love life
Who I am
What I teach
What I do
That's changing
Does it have to?
Will someone be brave
unafraid to leave tracks
allow strategy, for once,
to be first on a path
to right the wrongs that exist
in this place and time
To slam the door in tragedy's face
not mine Hold up
wait a minute
Is that knocking I hear
Is that tragedy saying,
"Strategy, nice to see you again dear."

I Can Die
I can die
In A Moment
a split Second
In the twinkling of an eye
Without time to cry
I can die
And it means
Nothing to nobody
Anything to anybody?
Something to somebody
who might cry, I surmise
Is that why, why I try
so hard to do right
to lose blindness for sight
to continue the fight
with all my might
and then some
before I die
(upon interruption)
One Breath
One small breath
is all it takes
to erase all that I am
all that I've done
all I've become
to those who care
One breath
One little breath
is all I need to breathe
the curse of death
and put me at rest
just one breath
There are days
when I tell myself.

Breathe

Flower of Beauty

Oh, flower of beauty

you take my breath away

literally

more and more each day

while comfortably surrounding

so many wreaths

you stand boldly

hiding deceit

behind your bright red and green

you carefully cover

dangers unseen

Flower of beauty

you take my breath away

as you remind me

of the value of each and everyday

Poinsettias are a sister plant
to the plant natural rubber latex is made from

Running
(high school graduation experience)

Running for my life
While running from my enemy
Running for my sake
While running from my support
Running for survival
While running from death
Running
just running

'Cause I'm trapped
cornered
with no clear way out
I'm searching
crumbling
fumbling about
I'm thinking
(No, I'm not)
"Just get out!
Get out!"

Be calm
"But I can't"
I'm so cold inside
running out of breath
dying
no place to hide

It hurts
Lord I'm tired
I want to stop
where I stand

But I can't
For there's warmth
Inside my right hand
The child's hand in mine
needs me by his side

So run
"But I can't"
from the fear in his eyes

Run
I can't
access denied

Running
Running for my life
While running from my enemy
Running for my sake
While running from my support
Running for survival
While running from death
Running just running

Life

There are times when I speak loudly
to deaf ears then shed tears,
'cause in their battle to help me
they stifle me
with their lack of understanding
while demanding I concede
to what they believe is best for me
knowing THEY DON'T KNOW
I try to control my mouth
before it heads south to my roots on my daddy's side
where women didn't try to hide
their thoughts when someone crossed
the line in their mind
that was sacred or simply their defense
sometimes I JUST NEED SPACE
to erase self-pity
from my vocabulary
'cause it has a way of creeping inside
attempting to hide in my heart
once I start to think
I sink rapidly
unabashedly
lower than low
How low can I go?
mmm... too low
I've fallen and I can't get up
'cause it's too much to bear
as people stare
while I walk away as they talk
handicapped anew with deafness
'cause though they try to help
the solution is for self
The problem needs to be resolved
so their life can evolve
to a level of comfort, I USED to have

before my valve rusted, maybe busted
due to built up pressure
of interrupting the plans of others
where they eat, sleep, run, play
interrupting their lives in every way
when I used to be invisible,
and that was comfortable for EVERYONE
Till now, I take a bow, as they insist
I comply with their wish
peace evades me if I stay
so, I walk faster and leave everyone in the dust
that I trust
to protect me and pause only for traffic
ignoring the laughing
of life, as life goes on for some

Hope Lives

My world is getting smaller
With every breath I take
I can disappear
in a moment
courtesy of someone else's small mistake
I want to live comfortably
I want to continually grow
I know this is possible
How so?
"For I know the plan that I have for You"
declared the Lord
"plans to give you hope and a future"
Jeremiah 29:11, that's the word
I hear
I receive
I believe it to be true
there's nothing God has promised
for which he won't give me the tools
Hope lives

Value

Value
every moment
every step
every word
every breath
they are not promised
aren't a given
aren't guaranteed
may not be blessed
can be taken
can be stolen
even kidnapped
can be denied
can be lost
in a split second
without due process
without a trial
and then
what do we value?
When we're stripped
of all our pride
stripped of our wishes
likewise denied
burdened down
thoughts interrupted
dreams deferred
left confused
unless we value
(Repeat from top)

The End?

I am
was
a change agent
(but in the wrong sense of the word)
I was changing simply because I was not heard
Whether I spoke softly or stood still and shouted
instead of a change agent
I'm in need of change
hesitating is doing nothing but causing me pain
breaking me
as some forsake me
squeezin' me, teasin' me
breathing stale air ceases
I fall into pieces
reaching the end
no the beginning
somewhat obscured
move forward
NO STOP

You're still unsure

Baby, grieve in your midnight
rejoice in your morn
it is death you are grieving
as you are reborn
the end
no more judging
the mirror awaits
as you turn loose your brother
to fess up and face
the end
NOPE
the beginning

Support

My mind
spinning
reeling
lost out in space
Wondering if what I see
is really taking place
The teachers, the nurses are all involved
making sure latex will not be allowed in
but I will be!
My ears are tingling
my toes are too
my heart is pumping
skipped a beat or two
I feel excited
can't catch my breath
this time
it has nothing to do with latex
thank you Lord, thank you Jesus
I want to shout
but could be thrown out
so, I must sit without wiggling
without making a sound
and hope my thoughts
aren't jumping around
too loudly
Finally, support

HESITANT...

TO PARENT

I was told, by a physician, I would never be able to have kids of my own. As one of six children myself, disappointment does not begin to describe how I felt. As a child I used to line up rocks, my pretend kids, and ask my mom to do their hair each night, after she did mine. She played along. Eventually I found peace in the fact that I already had children whose lives I could make a difference in. I was a public-school music teacher who saw hundreds of students each week. I was blessed.

Imagine my surprise when I found out I was pregnant. Excited doesn't even touch the sole of my emotions. I was twenty-eight years old when I had my daughter and thirty-six when I had my son. Married twice, divorced twice, (but that's for another book.) I ended up being a single parent for most of their lives! Parenting is no joke.

Born eight years apart, I told both Dominique and Kyle not to touch the water. The pictures demonstrate exactly how well that went! I know I made many mistakes as a parent but am forever grateful that my flaws did not prevent them from becoming amazingly creative, independent young adults. The poetry in this chapter was pulled from my childhood, my children's, and my parents, (as they aged, roles reversed.) Rhythmically playful, sometimes painful, always with a purpose, (laughter counts.)

Children

Children are a gift from God
their wide eye curiosity
mischievous smirks
dancing spirits
happy feet
Everything about them blesses us
comforts us
captivates and reminds us
of who we used to be
how we used to think
fears we used to face
and often the simplicity of life
For some of us it brings to the forefront
the child that remains deep inside
waiting for the adult
to admit that he or she still exists
waiting to grow up
be turned loose, consoled
that can only happen
when old memories are released
grudges forgiven
nicknames forgotten
deaths, dealt with
and we face up to who we really are
When you are in the company of children
allow yourself to be reminded of the simplicity of life
free from the chaos we face daily
see God through the eyes of a child
He is who he says he is
He does what he says he does
he lives inside each one of us
recall the simpleness of
"Jesus loves me this I know, for the bible tells me so"♪
Children are a gift

"I Want a Dad"

"I want a dad, a dad for me
At 10 months my dad left me
He stopped by four times, maybe five
since he left, I'm seven, surprise!

"I want a dad," my walk seemed to say
as I got into the car on a cold winter's day
My wanting a dad stuck in my mind
as we drove to school for the umpteenth time

"I want a dad." my secret for years
Don't want to hurt mom whose always here
No matter what I have to do
She always helps me to get through

"I want a dad." Raced through my head
The other day when my mom said
"Honey, what's wrong! You don't seem like yourself
I know we've talked but is there anything else?"

"I want a dad!" flew through the air
The words fled from my lips
while my eyes filled with tears,
I cried in a way I'd never cried before
I cried out the pain of seven Father's Days' maybe more
I cried out the hurt I feel hearing, "Hey dad!"
I cried for that something that I've never had
Then thought, "Oh no! Did I make mom sad?"
I thought it might hurt her, my wanting a dad

"I want a dad for you too," she replied
Dabbing with tissues the tears from my eyes
If you were to pick the right dad for you
What kind would you want if you were to choose?

I thought for a moment,
"A dad for me!"
Mmm... what would I want?
How should he be?
"Someone who would play with me,
someone who loved God
someone who would love
both me and you mom!"

My mom looked at me,
with my tears in her eyes
"I bet to Jesus honey that's no surprise
He knows what you want and won't send any less
than what He feels for you is the very best
Jesus knows your heart
and what's been on your mind
He'll answer those desires of yours right on time"

When we got to my school on that cold winter day
My mom and I
took a minute to pray
My heart felt better
I no longer felt sad
I knew my Father would comfort me
'till he sent my dad

Parenting

Parenting is not easy

Our children

are both precious and precocious

powerless and powerful

they constantly yearn to learn

the best way to get around us,

while working overtime to fluster us

help us lose our composure 10, 9 8, 7

Lord up in heaven meet me in this room

where danger looms

for the child that continues to push my buttons

I need everyone to pray

night and day without ceasing

(so this child won't defeat me)

"One day at a time, sweet Jesus,

That's all I'm asking of you ♪

Parenting is a trip

a journey

I never stop learning

to persevere

pray and praise

so, I can keep parenting

School

I love school
my teacher's nice
we do projects and have gym
I love school
we write
go home for lunch
come back again

"Oreo, Oreo!"

I like school
my art class
the poetry
I like to learn
I like school
math and reading
the awards that I earn

"Oreo, Oreo!"

While leaving school
kids pushed me
"Oreo" is what they said
School scares me
so do stitches
and the pain in my head
"Mama am I an Oreo?"
"No!" my mama said
But you are wonderfully
Beautifully and uniquely made
You are special
You're a child of God
And yes, you've been saved
I love school

A Lonely Child

A lonely child

may often cry

to make friends

they will tell lies

when the day

is long gone

they won't be able

to carry on

the lies come back

claw at their skin

a lonely child

cannot win

A lonely child

doesn't mean

an only child

Church Notes

(I found this conversation on an old church bulletin and couldn't resist including it. My children were not allowed to talk during church service and no gaming devices were allowed either. Dominique and Kyle are eight years apart in age. Cokoa was Dominique's cat.)

Dominique: Where's your DS?

Kyle: You don't want to know.

Dominique: In your pocket?

Kyle: Bingo!

Dominique: Oooooo! I'm telling! Well we can pictochat later. I don't know when though. Maybe if mom takes us out to eat, then we can do it.

Kyle: Please don't tell. I'll do anything, even feed Cokoa.

Dominique: Lol, I'm not going to tell on you Kyle! I was only playing.

Kyle: Do I still have to feed Cokoa?

Dominique: No Kyle... I don't think we're going to have time to go to grandma's today.

Kyle: But I want to feed Cokoa.

Dominique: So then I will show you how.
I can do it once a day and you can do it once a day.
I'm sure she will like that.

Kyle: Ya, bye

Dominique: Buh bye!

Child's Christmas Welcome

Once upon a time

on a dark but starry night

A baby boy was born

'neath the glow of a bright light

I'm told lambs 'baaed'

cows 'mooed'

while donkeys said hee-haw?

To welcome baby Jesus

On his bed made of straw

Well, I don't baa

I don't moo

Hee-haw I just won't say

But I do want to welcome you

on this blessed day

So I greet you with a smile

see right here on my lips

and floating out from my hand

a big holy kiss

Welcome!

Child's Offertory Prayer

We thank you for your goodness

We thank you 'cause we're here

We thank you for today, Lord

For one hundred thirty years

We thank you for the sunshine

We thank you for the rain

We thank you for the dollars

And we thank you for the change

We thank you Lord for blessing us

Each and every day

May this offering help people

Dear Jesus, I do pray

That those who had

gave happily and did the best they could

And those who did not have

will give to God by being good

I didn't want to do this

I hope my mom is pleased

This is my prayer dear Jesus

Thank you for hearing me

(130th church anniversary)

The Store

Once upon a time not long ago
my mama sent me to the store
Do you know what fo?
Ham, collard greens and black-eyed peas,
Now why is everybody lookin' funny at me?
My mama gave me a list and said, "Chile let's go.
and don't you spend the whole day
just a-walking to the store.
I want what I asked you for and nothing less,
You know I won't except anything less than your best?"

As I started to walk
I looked over the list
and thought, (very softly),
"Who does she think she is?"
I would never think out loud
never dare to speak,
the words I was thinking
as I walked down the street.
'Cause if momma said it once
you knew she meant what she said.
And you never talked back unless you wanted to be dead.
So, I knew what it was that I had to do.
I memorized the list to the rhythm of my shoes:

Ham, collard greens and black-eyed peas,
noodles, and milk, (for macaroni and cheese),
Lettuce and tomato for salad that's tossed
and Lawd have mercy some cranberry sauce.
Flour and sugar for biscuits and pie
Plenty of sweet potatoes, (now my feet began to fly).
Rice, turnips, turkey, and fresh green beans,
Now I'm startin' to get hungry, (If you know what I mean)

I can see the store! I'm almost there!
Oh no! All of a sudden, I become aware
of a sign
hangin' on the front door That says,
"Mama's supermarket ain't here no more."

Slowly I turn, I begin to sweat
I don't know what to do,
"Will Mama break my neck?"
"It wasn't my fault, mama will have to understand,
I'm 15 today! I'm a real woman."
So slowly I walk, step by step
Back to the house
My clothes soaked with sweat.
When I reached the front door
there was quite a surprise
An aroma filled the air my, my, my, my!

I smelled ham, collard greens and black-eyed peas,
noodles and milk, (macaroni and cheese!),
Lettuce and tomato, salad that's tossed
and Lawd have mercy some cranberry sauce.
Flour and sugar, biscuits, and pie
Oooh-wee sweet potatoes
(inside the house I fly).
Rice, turnips, turkey, and fresh green beans,
All that walking made me hungry
(if you know what I mean).

Inside the door loud voices greeted me
Singin' "Happy Birthday!"
"Could this really be?"
My mama set me up.
Boy she got me good.
But I got the last laugh
as I ate up all the food!

Triple S Threat
(A.k.a. Sunday School Struggle)

Sunday morning
alarm clock
beautiful
I'm up
blue sky
green grass
nice breeze
warm sun
Thank-you Jesus
Sunday morning!
Alarm clock's got my back
the only ones moving
me and our cat!
Daughter's sleeping
one foot hanging out
not hearing my voice
even when I shout
Son is still snoring
no covers in sight
though I shake, rattle & roll
to his pillow he holds tight
Sunday morning!
Rejoice! I hear in my head
as my children ignore me
asleep in their beds
The Sunday school struggle
has just begun
but I've got the Victory
battle's already won
I raise my voice
up another notch or two
now everybody's up
(Though looking confused)
"Does this match?"

"Look okay?"
"Can I borrow your blouse?"
"Mom, I can't find my shirt"
"It's nowhere in this house!"
"You must not have washed it"
"You said it'd be here"
"It's not my fault I'm not ready"
"I've got nothing to wear!"
Calmly I dress
then lay down the law
"I'm going, you can't stop me
and you'd better come along.
I don't want your excuses
You both know the deal"
The engine is started
my hands on the wheel
"Catch the car before it leaves
or you'll be riding the rail"
(and I'll have to pray
for help raising my bail)
Whew! We're all in the car
with no loss of limb
our focus off ourselves
now onto Him
The Sunday school struggle
coming to a close
We arrive at the church
safe and composed
We enter the sanctuary
feel the peace,
The spirit of kindness,
love that's released
We step forward to serve
with one heart,
one mind
The struggle was worth it
Victory is mine!

My Angels

Do I lose my angels if
my thoughts
walk
faults
are different than your own?

Do I lose my angels if
my goals
beliefs
views
and soul
are changing now that I'm grown?

Do I lose my angels if
my steps
regress
and become weaker than before
harder to restore?

Do I lose my angels if
my dreams
fall apart at the seams
and I feel
shattered to the core?

Do I lose my angels if
who I am becoming
doesn't agree
with whom you felt
I should be?

Do I lose my angels?
or
Are they mine permanently?

Brother-In-Training

My son sees you and watches
your walk
how you talk,
sit, hug,
even shake hands
He's a brother -in-training
you are teaching him to be a man

My son needs you to teach him
to tie his tie,
choose a hat,
maybe even get fitted for a suit,
To uplift him as he leaves being a youth
Sometimes even to reprimand
this young brother-in-training
You're teaching him to be a man

My son hears you and listens closely
as you speak to him,
and to one another,
Please understand
that what you say to
and about each other
this young brother-in-training
accepts as
what he needs to say
and do
to become a man

My son loves you for loving him first,
accepting him,

asking him about his grades,
school
and how he's feeling,
from him respect you all command
Yes
from this young brother-in-training
who's learning from you how to be a man

I ask you now
and pray that you understand
that I understand
you didn't ask for this responsibility
of helping my son become a man
but
this is a plea from a mother
for a brother
in-training
A plea for you, brothers
to come together and take a united stand
that will transport the young brothers of this community
Into becoming all that they can

I'm asking you
in love
to watch over each other
need each other
respect each other
pray for each other
and most of all
love each other, my brothers.

The Day Daddy Died

It stung the day my daddy died
The sting of his words
(like the sting of his death)
pierced my sides
rattled me
shook me
made me see
a different type of reality
through his eyes
"I lived my life in vain," he said
"I've done nothing that matters," burst into my ears
"My life was wasted," he said through his tears
"I worked hard for you kids," stabbed at my heart
"And now I'm dying," nearly ripped me apart
"And I lived for what" I heard through my tears
Anything else that was said on that day
fell on deaf ears
who have nothing to say
I think
I think often
on that day
of the things I could've
should've said
Hesitations...

Mom...Mother

A mom births a baby, a mother their burden bears
A mom consoles a baby,
a mother compassionately wipes away tears
A mom sees baby take its first steps, a mother
supports those steps with her soul and her breath
A mom, a mother

A mom loves when her child is right, a mother's love
understands they will also be wrong
A mom says goodnight, a mother's voice
caresses the night with a story or song
A mom tells a child there's no 'boogie man, a mother says,
"together let's pray"
and encourages her child to fear nothing
because of the love of Jesus,
because of her faith
A mom, a mother

A mom's pride points out her successful children, a
mother proudly watches them succeed
A mom's faith may wander and waiver, a mother
consistently believes, her child is not her own
but on loan to her from God
So, their trials, burdens, tears, steps
rights, wrongs, fears, breath,
challenges, failures, heartbreaks, success,
ALL belong to God

I am, who I am today because my mom
was, is and always will be my mother!

I'm Your Mother, Not Your Friend

I'm your mother, not your friend!
During my childhood those words made me mad
I resorted to moments of silence,
making people invisible and
ignoring attempts to make me laugh.
I mean the same exact words every time
my friends wanted to do something with me,
go somewhere without my siblings
Did the same song have to play again?
"Don't ask me why I said no,
I'm your mother, **not** your friend."

Adolescence wasn't much different
when it came to clothing or what I wanted to do
"How ma-ny times do I need to re-mind you?
I'm your mother, not your **friend**"
I guess the remix was simply
where the emphasis was placed
Through how many of life's stages
was it necessary for those words to assault my ears?
At this age, leaving me in tears
It was then that I made up my mind
I would **never** be a mother, they were simply unkind
They didn't understand how times had changed
They were stuck in the past only one song in their brain
I would not be a mother, if anything, I'd be a mom
They were cool, less rigid and had more fun
I couldn't wait to get out and be on my own
No mother to tell me what time to be home

Many years later with two children of my own
made it through their childhood and adolescence
singing my mother's song

I'm your mother, NOT your friend
Even in those moments when their eyes filled with tears
I remembered those were the times
I learned how to persevere

Knocked down, ego bruised
Found my way back up
despite my countless mistakes
given unconditional love

Minus my blinders of personal wisdom,
I remember how my mother danced
the faces she made as she read to my children
how she wiggled for them
(as if she had ants in her pants!)
I remember her laughing
until tears wet her cheeks
I remember her singing
hymns while she cleaned
how early she woke
how late she went to bed
how worn her bible was
and priceless things she said

In Proverbs 31:26 it says
"She opens her mouth in wisdom
and the teaching of kindness is on her tongue"
It took me until adulthood to realize
my mother hadn't gotten this wrong!
Your mother is your best friend for life!
but only once you're grown,

Leaves in July

My mother
raked leaves in July
I think as I cry
I stand in the rain
trying to erase the pain
of the picture
permanently
etched in my brain
of my mother
raking leaves in July

How would I have known
that it would be
the last time in our history
that we would spend
outside together
(other than someone's facility)

That day
she would not stop
would not leave
one leaf on the ground
I still hear the sound
of her
raking leaves in July

Now here I stand
I rake leaves in December
My kids don't understand why
I don't want one leaf
left on the ground

I rake
trying to erase the sound
of my mother
raking in July

I rake leaves
in December
I stand in the rain
trying to release the pain
of my mother and I
in July

If only I had done better
there would not have been leaves
to rake in July
my mother and I
could have spent our time together
talking
laughing
singing
remembering

Had I been up to par
she would not have gone so far
as to rake leaves
in July
Will the pain ever subside?
70+ bags later
I still see leaves
so
I rake leaves
in December
why?
Because my mother
raked leaves in July

Mother's Day

Last year concerns were here
but mother was still near
her hum
stories
opinions

It was easy to reach for her
walk with her
talk with her too

Then without being warned
(I'd like to believe)
her presence was gone

In the blink of an eye,
she needed more care
it was possible she'd die

I thought I was independent
I thought I was grown
I thought I didn't need any earthly being
At least that was my song
now "I sing because I'm happy ♪"
no longer feels right
"I want Jesus to walk with me ♪"
replaced it in one night

Dementia With Psychosis

Mother,

I'll answer the doorbell

that's not ringing

Get off the phone

I'm not on

Talk to the people

who aren't talking to me

See nighttime

at the crack of dawn

Get dressed

when it's not time to do so

Eat burgers

with jelly or jam

Dance to the music

that's not playing

Be whoever

you say that I am

Just to

have you once again

HESITANT
TO CHANGE

Experiencing all four seasons is one of the benefits of continuing to live in Connecticut. I love watching trees naturally change colors and when reduced to bareness, become reborn again. Stronger as each new year approaches and then the cycle repeats smoothly. There's a pattern, a rhythm to it.

Unlike the trees, I struggle with change. Changing bad habits like procrastination, dealing with the physical and emotional changes of my body (accepting those thighs!) Changes in relationships, and not just love. The fact that their leaves will only be there for a season doesn't hinder the growth or cycle of the tree.

Why then is it so hard to realize the same is true for me? Those size 5's that I began my teaching career in, were for a season! Wanting things to change without speaking or taking action towards it, should never have been a season. Living in a, I should do less so you can be more mentality, another bad season. Knowing that speaking your truth may reduce long term relationships to leaves scattered on the ground, like in the fall, never to be reclaimed, is a season new to me. One that is causing me to be reborn stronger and with new leaves.

Changing

I'm changing!
Why?
Should I be?
I thought I could just stay the way I am...
(or should I say was?)
for the rest of my life
But,
I am finding that I cannot
So, where do I go from here?
Shall I remain in hiding
or will I become the adult that I am supposed to be?
Decisions,
decisions
Friends are they really my friends
or are they just images that I create to please myself?
Also...
are they any better off than I am
or do I just make them seem that way?
Once again,
decisions...
This time I will decide
I will find out for myself,
who I am
what I believe
and what that means for my future
I will discover me,
learn to love me
thus, I will free myself
and
be

What Makes Me Curious?

A sound

a smell

an unusual word

Something different

something I've never heard

a picture

or title

that sparks an idea

something that grabs me

something that makes me feel

up

or down

or simply the same

what makes me curious?

Change

Wake Up!

Wake up!

Please won't you wake up

I need you

I don't want to be alone

and

I wasn't

that is,

until you fell asleep

Wake Up!

Please!

it's only when you are completely awake

that I feel the warmth and searching in your eyes

the full effects of your smooth dark hair

the little twitch that wiggles your nose and your smile

the smile that says a million words

about loving,

caring

and needing me

Wait!

I'm the one who's asleep

I Wish

I wish I was invisible

to the naked eye

I wish it was impossible

for anyone to see me cry

I wish I was invisible

to all who sought me out

I wish that on my darkest days

my thoughts I could drown out

I wish

Fix Me

"Oh, oh fix me" ♪

Why am I weeping?

My heart is heavy

while my lips are praising

"Oh, oh fix me" ♪

The tears fall quickly

as I sit crying

while my feet are dancing

"Oh, oh fix me" ♪

My eyes are closing

while water's flowing

as rejoicing enters my soul

it's refreshing

my toes are tapping

"Oh, oh fix me" ♪

Letting Go

Letting go of the past isn't easy

Every direction I turn to

something else pops out

to scare me

to chase me

to tempt me to turn away

from that which sustains me

letting go

things oozing through my fingers

seeping

through the cracks of my toes

dripping from my eyelids

letting go

let go

whoa

feels good

Talk

I talk

But there's no one there

Though the room is full
of love and care

Still

there's no one there
that can hear
me talk
or cry

I ask
why
no cloth can wipe
away my tears
(that aren't there)
although they flow
everywhere
inside
As I cry
silently

Although you know
you do not see
or hear
or feel
the me that's here
the me that's real

Why talk?

What Do You See?

What do you see when you look at me?

Do you see me for who I am

or who you 'heard' I would be?

Am I too tall or too short?

Too fat or too thin?

(I just couldn't resist slipping that last one in)

Is it my walk, my talk, or my color at birth

that you've been trained to spot as a character flaw first?

Do you see a young girl?

An old woman to be?

Just what is it you see when you first look at me?

A person who's happy and armed with a smile?

(But deep down inside is a frightened child?)

When I look in the mirror I'm all of my dreams

There are no boundaries, I'm a model or a queen

but that vision disappears, fades from view

when while you look at me, I look at you

R U Uncomfortable?

R U uncomfortable with your eyes
your back side
your personality
reality
your looks
how you cook
your thighs?

R U uncomfortable with your walk
your talk
your lips
your hips
your nose
your clothes
your thighs?

R U uncomfortable with how you act
how you're stacked
what wiggles
your giggle
your hair
what's up there
your thighs?

R U uncomfortable with your sister
your brother
your father
your mother
your spouse
or significant other
and those thighs?

Feeling Grown

I'm 21, feeling grown,

independent

and on my own

A teacher in a white preschool,

no looking back,

life is cool

I look good, got enough money...

My life is fine

I thought,

til I heard,

"Nigger would you tie my shoe?"

Whooo! That blew my mind!

Rudely awakened from my dream life

I didn't know what to say

If Erin had been more than 3,

my fist might have had its way.

I said, "Erin, you know that's not my name.

I'm really surprised at you."

Erin, looked genuinely confused and said,

"But that's what Mommy and Daddy call you."

The Young Black Man

The young black man struggles to be

struggles to live in peace

in this society

Who can he turn to

if there's no one there?

When he cries for help

does anyone hear

or do we simply turn our backs and say,

"You know, honey chile,

I knew he'd turn out that way.

For that is what black men are all about

you know doin' wrong

and hangin' out

Have you ever known one that was any good?"

How can it be that the black man is so misunderstood?

I

I speak with none understanding

I cry out to those with no ears

I dance in the presence of no one

In front of the blind, I silently shed tears

I wonder why there's no answer

I wonder, then wonder some more

I stand paralyzed, hands glued to my side

Staring at an unopen door

"Yield," I whisper silently

The sound drifts before it impacts

the parts of me that could make a difference

gone before I can act

So, I talk after everyone's left me

(Repeat from top)

Paralyzed By Possibility

Paralyzed

I stand

traumatized

by the demand to move forward

What if I move

and I miss?

I lose

That which I was reaching for drifts away

from my grasp

when at last

I try

Paralyzed I sit

and simply wish

I could leap

from my seat

and attempt to use

the child of my blues

to encourage others

my sisters and brothers

I have possibility

that paralyzes me

Fragments

Fragmented ideas
to be or not?
Does it matter?
To Whom?
Cross your t's
check your dots

Why?
What's the point?
Does it count?
Why? Why not?

Fragments
floating
crashing
afraid to drop
opinions
that differ
thoughts that may make
the fragments
more fragmented
my presence
a mistake

Particles of negativity
pricking my mind, ouch
I so value
every moment of time
that I have left
Does this matter?
Is it worth

my minutes?
My breath?
Breathe
(sigh)
Breathe again

Fragments gently
becoming whole

Breathe
fresh breath
mmm.... feels so good

A divine appointment
a revelation
knowing
I should be here
My voice matters
I am part of change
thought provoking
discussions
no status quo
I won't leave as I came

Firm steps
defined direction
time to move doubts aside
and move
towards my purpose
in confidence
glide baby, glide

Speak On

Speak to me

loudly,

clearly

vision crystalizing

as I hear thee

feel your presence

the essence

soothed me,

groomed me

healed me

as it freed me

Speak on

Guide me

firmly

deliberately

help my feet

move

in a new groove

as I grow

closer to thee

prophecy

pipe dreams

fill me,

heal me

seal me,

free me

Speak on

Strengthen me

quickly

completely

overcoming all of me

I need thee desperately

control me

so I see

optimally

who I am supposed to be

believe

receive

freely thee

Speak on

Chains

The chains that bind me
blind me
to self
I look around and see no one else
but me
holdin' the key
to my relationship with you
What will I do?
Your word
I've heard
too many times
to close my mind
and think that will stop
the Holy spirit from comin' in and pickin' the lock
to my heart and soul
worth more than gold
to the devil
I know I am convicted
'cause it's already been scripted
re-run
been done

So the chains that bind me
can no longer blind me
to the truth
that's in pursuit
of me
and me of it...

Jesus you win
and so do I
devil get thee
behind
me
Got some chains here 'for free!

I Am Inspired

I am inspired
though awful tired
as I sit on the edge
of a ledge
of the window of opportunity
that has no boundaries

I gaze
somewhat dazed
by all I can see
that can be
part of an unbelievable future...
not needing sutures
that calls
then stalls
when I try to start
the part
that was not mine to touch
but belongs to Jesus
who has a mission
through visions
he reveals
has me feel (and makes real)
When I move completely out of the way
and remember there to stay

Yes inspired,
full of desire
to serve
though I don't deserve
to do so
You know
I am enlightened
though sometimes frightened
by the edge
of the ledge
on which I sit
feeling not fit
or worthy of
though God above
sees me
differently

So I leap
ready to reap
all that He calls me to grasp
despite my past
to claim
in His name
I am enlightened

Times

There are times self-designed

this minute I'm in it

and all I want to do is cry

as my mind screams WHY?

Cry out loud, scream and shout

'cause I'm tired, worn, weak and forlorn

I think, I'm too tired to cry

too wired to allow myself to give in

I'm fine (no I'm not)

but the tears simply will not drop

afraid they won't stop

if they start to depart from the part of me

that has sheltered them for so long

(No matter how wrong that may be)

Please let me be

There are times like now

when I want to take a bow

and then exit stage left

to reappear as the me that's not here

the woman I desire to be in thee

please set her free

now, wow

there she is!

Live With Intent

Live with intent
that is intend to live
with each second that passes we have so much to give
To not do so is a sin
(as in **S**itting, **I**nvariably, **N**eglectful) of our purpose
That is not allowed if we are to devour
our purpose in life
We must strive to complete the goals that sit at our feet
glide in our stride as each day passes by
whispering
calling
sometimes shouting
our name as they sit in pain
neglected
disrespected
while we talk about dreams
we don't allow to be seen
or the plan we won't dare
put pen in hand to write down
which leaves our goals in a frown
So, what's next?
Is it time to put our intent to the test
and see what truly is to be, or not to be?
For that is the question that leaves me
perplexed and seeking direction
while praying to be blessed
with answers before
I step to the door, step out on faith
wanting cement to already be placed
under my feet so I can't fall or fail
so there can't be surprises
no unknowns in this life
the journey to live with intent or intend to live
each minute, each second, giving all I can give
to life, to dreams that I intend to fulfill

It Is Easy & You Can Choose

It is easy to feel dark when darkness is all around you
It is easy to lose hope when hopelessness surrounds you
It is easy to become negative
when negativity is all you hear
It is easy to become scared
when all you see in others is fear
It is easy to lose sight
when the blindness of others guides your way
It is easy to speak foolishly
when that's all you hear others say
It is easy to feel unlovable
when those closest to you don't show love
It is easy to doubt God
when storms received are perceived from above
It is easy to be poor
when money is your God
It is easy to fail
when you think that you don't know how
It is easy to stop dreaming
when you're surrounded by broken dreams
It is easy to give up
when no one chooses you for their team
It is easy to stop trying
when no one suggests you should try
It is easy to stop breathing when you're told you will die
It is easy to frown when sadness lives on your street
It is easy to sit frozen
when tiredness bathes your weary feet
It is easy to feel ugly
when no one's ever said you're not
It is easy to crave death
when you don't know that you've got
a purpose, a dream to fulfill
that you were created with something
called free will

You can choose to see past your surroundings and pain
You can choose to stand strong
despite the rain
that leaves tracks on your face
that refuse to dry
You can choose to move forward,
you can choose not to die
You can choose to be beautiful
and speak hope everyday
and encourage others around you
so they might see the way
to a world within a world that's full of positivity
You can choose to see past all the negativity

You can choose to stand
though those around you lay down
You can choose to share a smile
when all that's meeting you is frowns
You can choose to be different,
you can choose to be whole
You can choose the destiny
of your life and your soul
You can choose to be rich
when all around you are broke
You can choose to be content
with what you have not constantly hope
for bigger or new material things to rain down on you
You can stand when others fall if you choose
You can choose

Right vs. Wrong

We all have a choice
we all have the chance
to use our voice
when we stand
at the crossroad
a choice to make
when we stand at a fork wondering
which road to take
Shall we follow in the footsteps
of those long gone
who stood for justice
and not for what's wrong
when it means we will hurt
those whom we love
or will we cave to the pressure
and give righteousness a shove

Abuse the privilege of the position we hold
Abuse our liberty, abuse all we've been told
of the love of Jesus and how to do what is right
we abuse Calvary in order to sleep at night
with the devil
who pleases our earthly lust
who seduces us physically
who betroths us to unjust
illogical behavior
that can't be denied
the truth peeks through our words daily
no matter how hard we try
to cover it
truth prances between our words

dances across our actions
and cries to be heard
so we bury it deeper,
cover it with more dirt
and ignore the voice that says,
"too many will be hurt!"
'cause we'll sacrifice it all
in order to stay
in the moment
in the lie
truth get out my way
Doesn't matter how many paths get erased
Or the fact it may impact those we embrace
Right vs. wrong
we all must choose
which we value more
who we might have to lose
to preserve what's left of our integrity
what's left of our faith,
our honesty
our choice decides
our eternal home
Truth will sing to the glory
of all those done wrong
she will crow like a rooster
facing a new dawn
while standing at the crossroad
of night vs day
Truth, though it may take time,
will have her way

Time

Time

We take time to what?

To discuss time

Singing time, playing time

But it's taking time, to talk about time

and my mind is

floating, toting too much other stuff

that has to be done

(that could be more fun)

A more fun use of huh, my time

Time to think, time to read

time to be who I be.... come

When

I have the time

to create, play or simply stay

in one spot and stop

to feel time movin' by

Time

In Order To

I've been praying for God to reveal
the reason for the trials I've been going through...
Why would he bring me this far
(through all the hell that I've been through)
put me so close
to what seemed like victory over the devil
the demons in my life
and then...
have me feel pain worse than anything I've ever known?

In order to feel worthy
I believe I had to be brought down to the very bottom...
I thought I had hit it, but I hadn't...

In order to feel beautiful
I had to feel absolute ugliness
and see it in my reflection...
I now appreciate the beauty you've always seen in me

In order to feel capable
I had to be rendered completely helpless!
Not able to walk, talk, feed or care for myself
All I could do was cry and moan
I now appreciate every ability, gift and talent
I've been blessed with

In order to feel intelligent
I had to reach a point of not knowing anything,
not a clue which way to go or what to do
Forming a complete sentence was a challenge
I now appreciate being able to speak
and don't take it for granted
I had to change

HESITANT
TO FEEL

Feel, a small word that carries so much weight. Early on I was taught not to feel, and if I did feel something, not to let the world know. If people knew how you felt, they knew how to control you. You should never let anyone control you. This isn't something that was ever said to me. It was learned through a child's eyes, a child's observations. I saw what happened when the teacher brought out crayons and someone yelled out, "I want the orange one!" The child closest to the crayon box would immediately choose orange. The child who called out sat defeated. **Lesson learned never let people know what you really want.**

I wanted to feel beautiful, talented, athletic, smart and funny like my siblings Fredrecia, Toya, Renée, Ricky and Vinny. Those were the words used to describe them, but never me, (when I listened in on adult conversations.) Because I did not hear them, I assumed those were attributes I did not have. **Lesson learned if someone doesn't speak into existence the qualities you desire, you don't have them, and never will.**

Another lesson through my childhood eyes was when someone called you something that wasn't your name and tears were shed, that became a weapon that would be used against you consistently. **Lesson learned never cry when someone's words hurt you.**

Feeling loved was important to me but I'm not sure what I thought indicated whether I was loved or not. I focused on my shortcomings and high, (sometimes impossible,) expectations that I imposed on myself, as a love meter. For example, being a straight A student wasn't good enough, I needed an A+ in every class. Then I would feel loved. When I achieved that goal my focus went to my next imperfection. I was overweight. So, if I became slim like my brothers and sisters, then I would feel loved. I don't know why I felt there was something you had to do to earn love, but I did. **Lesson learned it is possible to feel like you're failing when you're not.**

These early lessons went with me into adulthood. They might explain how I ended up married without ever having a man hold my hand, (except for on the way out of the church, after we were pronounced man and wife.) They also might explain why I ended up divorced. Don't get me wrong, my husbands, (yes there were two,) were not perfect. They were however, married to a woman that never voiced what she really wanted. One who would not make a decision about something, but then resent the decision that was made. A woman who needed to hear positive attributes about herself spoken, to believe she possessed them. A woman who would not cry when actions or words hurt her, which sometimes made her appear cold. A woman who felt like she was failing as a wife even though she later found out, she wasn't.

Becoming aware of my emotions has been a long process. I've had to deal with abandoned feelings along the way, but it was worth it. Lessons learned: One's perceptions control their actions. A person who doesn't love themself, is difficult to love. A person who has not accepted themself, is difficult to accept. A person who has not dreamed cannot survive with a dreamer.

I am a dreamer. This section gives glimpses into how I feel about the past, present and future.

Free to Feel

Freedom to sing

what I couldn't speak

gave freedom to my thoughts

and freedom to my dreams

Physically in bondage...

mind miles away

music, my saving grace...

I'm the American slave

Freedom in my faith,

while trapped in my tears

gave birth to spirituals

and hope through the years

Hummed while I worked,

whistled to become whole

Though softly I sang

freedom shouted through my soul

Freely I danced

while outwardly still

Free in the music... Free to feel

Love
(an educator's perspective)

Love
a short word with a long reach
that is the foundation of what we do daily
teach

It touches
bleeds
explores
exceeds
breathes
new life into everything that matters

I know love by its touch
(even when we can't)
it's there in the eyes
that stare
expressively
warmly
tearfully
nearly speaking a language of their own
over the masks
whispering you are not alone

Love
a short word with a long reach
in every breath we continue to take
even when struggling to breathe
for ourselves
that's love

I Love You (♪lyrics)

I have feelings I don't understand

I close my eyes and you are there

without making a sound

your name slips from my lips

I have grown to miss you

When all for the day is said and done

I return to my room wondering why

a part of me is still aching inside

I have grown to need you

When we are in the midst of a crowd

I can see us alone

I feel emotions, vibrations

traveling back and forth

I shiver because I want you

And now as I sit alone in my room

knowing you no more than yesterday

I realize I miss you

need and want you

all because I love you, from afar

You Just Can't Understand

You know what?
I love you!
I love you more than you could ever know
more than my words or my actions could show
Yes, so much more
But
I can't tell you because I was married before
Our past is something you prefer we not discuss
You said, "Let's not go there,
let's concentrate on us."
That's hard sometimes for me
for there are things that I know you can't understand
because you don't know where I've been
(or what I thought was a man)
Sometimes I want to shout out loud
(the wrongs you've made right)
I rejoice instead, silently
in the safety and warmth, I feel at night

How I want to tell you this
and so much more
But
I can't tell you
even though you know I was married before
It's not that I am trying to compare the two of you
for I know that won't get me anywhere
It's just that what I feel now
is so very new
and I've noticed how much that seems to surprise you
I can clear up the mystery of who I am
If you'll just let me tell you where I've been
(and what I thought was a man)

Afraid

I'm so scared!!
Afraid of illness, afraid of death
Afraid of making my fears known,
and most of all,
afraid for myself.
I'm looking for someone who will hold my hand,
If I mention fear (to those who have raised me)
I am chided like the child I used to be
Lord knows, it only makes me more afraid
I must be strong,
for no one can know what really goes on
inside of me, the worrying, the chaos, the searching, the crying
and most of all the hurting.
Surprisingly enough!
The pain is not all from the illness itself.
but from the hands that have gone cold,
just as my hands begin to seek warmth.
Still
I approached you
you listened, (or kind of listened),
and then (as though a cue had been given)
you spoke
spoke of oh so many things!
But not the matter that was on hand.
WHY CAN'T YOU HEAR ME?
I need you,
Just for a moment
Just one kind word
Oh the wonders that could have been done
with one little hug. It would have been half my cure.
But you, (off in some other world,)
walked away
Left me one step behind where I began
I approached you (the group of you)
you heard, yes you listened, and thought, (or so I thought),
then spoke.

But not of cures or good wishes to be bestowed
You spoke in riddles and many private jokes,
It was then that I began to laugh
Now the laughter doesn't come at all
Not even the fake kind
It's gone for good
The laughter has been replaced with pain.
Pain that makes tears fill my eyes,
so that I can no longer see
and once they are there
they sit
Afraid to fall
Afraid to show that they are real
Afraid the path they leave,
might cause others to follow,
and yes,
afraid of going through
whatever they might chance
to fall down upon
Even more afraid they might somehow fall and yet
leave no trace!
Leave no mark at all
because.........
I do not cry I am strong!
Yet here I sit,
I'm so scared
Afraid of illness, afraid of dying,
So afraid of making my fears known
and even more afraid for myself.
So now I come to YOU,
The one I should have sought the moment I became afraid.
Please dear Lord!
see me through, for I am afraid

Save Her

Someone please save her before it's too late
She is so far gone she feels life is through
Her pain and hunger are driving her away
Toward things she swore she'd never do

Contrary to the belief that she has a good home
(which is a well-known fact to all around)
She is really walking through this world alone
Her prison is her home, she's lost and down.

She started out with dreams no one could steal
Now has a world of trouble on her mind
Even though she can no longer feel
She still, (when she remembers), greets life with a smile.

Known outside as good and inside feeling pure evil
She has her reasons, (we all know that),
She has, (for some time), been sleeping with the Devil
Finding tears even though she is seeking laughs.

Love for her is an unseen thing
which for those who know better is such a shame
And this girl, she is just seventeen!
that in itself, fills some hearts with pain.

She is headed for trouble, spiraling down
with empty eyes that no longer see
She has learned to deceive without makin' a sound
She's lost love, life, dreams, and reality.

Alone she has driven herself to madness
Often at night she hangs her head to cry
If only she could come to her senses
Some of her dreams might be kept alive.

She lives in chains, not knowing she has the key
All too often she needs a strong one
She'll be fine as soon as she believes
Music will compose her a victory song

She only sees life from high on a cloud
Save her please before it's too late
She is one loose leaf hangin' on autumn's bough
She will never find the future if she hesitates

Someone please save me before it's too late
Please wake me up! No! Bring back my dreams
Because in her I alone patiently wait
Is life ever what it really seems?

IF

If, what if
I looked as I did way back then?
Would you? Could you? Love me completely again"
If my hips weren't as rounded
and my thighs not as full,
would you see? Could you see?
Right through the wool that is covering your eyes
rendering them blind
to the love that is unconditionally yours
the love that is mine 'cause
I love you
despite the hair that's turned gray
despite the reflection that greets me where hair once
blocked the way
despite the new width of your body, the illness that
attacks your sight which is failing
my love is intact
your smile speaks volumes to my heart like nothing else
can
my heartbeat quickens when I dream of you as my man
BUT
I won't beg you to stay or dig deep inside
to determine who would, who should be your bride
I love you
from the depths of my soul
My love is more precious than mountains of gold
Would you, could you if I looked as I did
would you, could you love me again?

Darkness

Darkness
The darkness of drug addiction, depression, infidelity
The darkness of envy, fear of violence, confused sexuality
Darkness
darkness
The darkness of gang life, peer pressure, everyday fears
The darkness of death, no discipline,
no direction and heavy tears
Darkness, darkness....
It **is** in darkness
that depression is found
courted by lack of direction
(which entered without making a sound)
But then rejoiced in the darkness
blindly shooting and stabbing our hearts
Boldly looting our spirits...
leaving us in the dark...
Darkness

If we're honest...
Darkness has entered the hearts
of many of us in this room
Darkness along with despair, despondency and gloom

Darkness,
The demon who removes all sight
Darkness,
Who comes as a thief in the night
to steal our dreams, our desires, even our vision
then leaves us drowning in strife, illness and conviction
Defeated, discouraged, distressed and weak
darkness entered our hearts and its symptoms were seen
As lack of direction gave way to our need to belong
our leaning towards right took a detour towards wrong.
Darkness.

How Can I

How can I be honest
and not risk being hurt
How can I admit what I'm thinking
and not lose sight of God's Word
How can I allow my feelings
to surface at their will
How can I feel like flying
when my brain is yelling "be still"
How can I control my longing
to feel you in my arms
How can I stop the wondering
if my heart will be harmed
How can I face tomorrow
if I won't deal with feelings from today
How can I stop hesitating
and step forward on faith
How can I allow your lips on mine
to control all my thoughts
How can I feel so complete with you
and then so totally lost
In my desire to run my fingers
through the hairs upon your chest
then slowly bring them upward
your face and neck to caress
How can I want to risk it all
knowing the pain of my past
How can I know that there's no choice
'cause my heart is beating fast

How do I know it's because of you?
'Cause you control the speed
of my heart, steps I take
the tempo of the air I breathe
How do I know that you're worth
me taking the risk

I know by the way my body tingles
every time we kiss
My knees wobble, I grow faint
Your lips feel like my own
in sync, entirely
The inner peace mmm, pleasant tone
How do I know we're meant to be
'cause with you I don't need to ad lib
Eve has become my middle name
And we're connected by the rib

Mmm. Mmm, Mmm!

I sit
telling my will to be still
But...EVERY PART OF ME wants to jump up and scream
this isn't a dream
You sit at a distance
as I sit wishin'
it was okay
to sit closely today
I'm impatient to feel your arms surround me, tenderly
providing the safety, I so desperately need
as my heart skips a beat
praying the moment could be preserved
as I float on the words
that drift from your lips
(which I wish
could touch mine)
anytime
I wanted them to
You are so fine
mmm,
I'm watching you from behind
Broad shoulders
for holdin' me up
when devilish stuff
tries to attack

Broad shoulders attached
to a firm chest and muscular back
my hands long to caress
from the base of your neck
to the base of your spine
one muscle at a time
until the light turns green
and we face each other seeing
love in our eyes
that can't be denied
A God sent love, from up above
deeper than anything we've ever felt
A chance we've been dealt
to share ourselves
in a way that Jesus permits
as I submit
myself to you
Mmm, mmm, mmm!

Sleeping With The Devil

Sometimes I wonder if I'll ever be the same

I just can't believe you'd dog me so

cause so much pain

I wish just for one moment you could feel what I feel now

Then you'd know the pain your gestures cause,

you'd understand how

How I could feel beaten, how I could feel abused,

how I could feel misled, how I could feel used.

I've given you my affection,

I've trusted you with my dreams

I've thrown all caring to the wind, I threw aside my beliefs

in God... I was too busy to take a stand

Too busy hoping you would be my man

I've run the distance in caring, in sharing your concerns

I've tried to be supportive and been there at every turn

You've hurt me... I let you but that doesn't make it right

You've hurt me, its true yet you sleep through the night

Without a care in the world a quite comfortable fellow

I guess it never hit me

I'd been sleeping with the devil!

Love You Enough

I've got to love you enough to let you fall
If my love is truly all
(that I say it is)
Then as much as it hurts
I've got to let go
I know
Your mom knows
Your dad knows
Your friends know
Everyone but you
Knows the worth of the love of a good woman
the benefits it brings a deserving man
but you don't understand
the heights to which together we could climb
the dreams we could reach
you prefer to be left behind
clinging to what was
or what could have been
living in past glories
not creating any since
accepting love that will bring you down
painting your name negatively all about town
mixed with sugar daddy love
which won't support you
when crises come your way
they won't know what to do
or care to
I love you
enough to let you fall

Pure

I want to have a pure heart

but don't know where to start

don't know why I desire

to have my fire

lit by you

if the truth be told

I've prayed from the depths of my soul

for us to be

what I see

in my dreams

and seems

to be a perfect match

A pure heart

pure mind

pure motive

pure design

love is so blind

Bad All By Myself

I can do bad all by myself.
I don't need help from anyone else
So before you get placed on that there shelf
You need to remember that if nothing else.
"I DON'T GIVE A S......."
Is ringin' in my ears
I still see a look of lunacy in your eyes,
A look that said, "you better go somewhere!"
Well baby,
I ain't movin'
I ain't runnin'
And I won't hide
If that hurts your feelings
Then maybe your feelings should step aside
'Cause I am not happy!
"Achoo!"
(I know you heard me sneeze, but you don't have to say
anything for God to bless me.)
He's blessed me with sense
to know when enough is enough
Tonight baby was strike two,
Your turn at bat is almost up,
Yes I love you
But I don't like you anymore
What made me feel so good and loved is long gone
You used to respect me
Now you're comfortable cursing in my face
It doesn't seem to matter if the kids are asleep or awake!)
You used to listen to me
Now a sentence I can't speak
Why? Are your words more important,
more important than listening?

Think twice my friend
this simply will not do
I won't back down to anyone
and the Lord will see me through
Do you realize all I sacrificed
to walk with you down the aisle?
It was not a simple gesture,
This was meant to last awhile
However, that can change
'cause I won't be driven insane
By a yelling, cursing demon,
who as an alias uses your name
I did not marry you for money
we both know that's not the case
I married you because I thought
together we'd run this race
I did not marry you, kind sir,
just to raise my self esteem
For I already know
I'm a chosen and blessed child of the King
What I've noticed lately is the price I've begun to pay
For every sacrifice I make, two more are on the way
Check out my before list, look at my after
You write the ending for this bittersweet chapter
My health was good, my weight okay
regular checkups all I needed
Now I feel like I live on medicine
and my closest friends are diseases
The next time you feel like cursing me
Baby, think twice
Your turn at bat is almost up
you've got 3 balls, 2 strikes
What happens next you won't be able
to blame on anyone else
I don't need anybody to bring me down...
I can do bad all by myself

Finally Love Me

I love you but not just as a friend

can't be your buddy, co-conspirator, confidant and then

sit waiting for your words and actions

to become visible truths to you

while my all is on the line

clinging to your nothing to lose

mentality

It's not easy to open old wounds

so they can heal properly

and allow us to feel loved and accepted

without fear of rejection or abuse

(which we readily use as an excuse

to hide from new harm)

My love will never be enough

Too much has transpired

for your words to make your heart a liar

I finally love me enough

to let you go

A Fragmented Heart

A fragmented heart beats irregularly

often a rhythm that no one can feel or hear

although the tears flow consistently

soak the breast of the vest

that clothes the heart

that stops and starts often

hurt, a fragment

jealousy, a fragment

spite, a fragment

pain, a fragment

loneliness, a fragment

death, a fragment

my fragmented heart

beats irregularly

in me

If Only

If only you could see inside

if only you could hear

if only healing could take place

if only you were aware

if only I could touch you again

If only I could feel

If only I could see the truth

If only I'd be real

If only I had had more sleep

if only I believed

If only I had listened more

I might not have been deceived

if only I was more beautiful

if only I was more clean

If only I could accept

my if's

wouldn't have changed a thing

Sing Me a Lullaby (♪lyrics)

Someone hold me and sing me

a lullaby,

a lullaby,

a lullaby

so I won't cry.

Please let me be,

the woman you once saw in me

know that I understand

like you I feel the pain

the pain that comes

when two become one

and then two again.

I know your place has been

with me right from the start

Lying deep within,

the chambers of my heart

now the time has come

its over

and we're two again

But somehow when you opted to leave

all too much of you remained

here inside of me.

And although we talk but never speak

I still hear everything you say to me.

I care for you and always will

no matter where we go,

Or what we choose to do

after all we've been through.

Oh, I know that you

my first love will always be true.

So, someone hold me and sing me

a lullaby,

a lullaby,

a lullaby,

to dry my eyes

to calm my heart

to make me one again

Why?

Why do I feel so hurt?
Why?
Some days it seems like it doesn't take much
It can simply be the lack of touch
that bruises me in places unseen
then leaves me in-between
where I am
and
where I desire to be

The more I try to do what's right
the harder it seems I have to fight
to remain in place
to run this race
I love you
but you
hurt me consistently so
I must go
to the only place
I know that is safe
A place where I will be protected
my feelings respected
Is that place for me,
me alone
on my own
with Christ?
Then I stand
accused of shutting others out
who stand and shout
about
my need to interact more,
share, be open, think with an open door
about relationships
that will be no more
I know why

Family

Six **single** letters
that attempt to define
what we are,
when **connected**
ironic, isn't it?
Blows my mind
Huh, most of us spend a lifetime
searching to create,
describe, or re-state
what makes up a family?
I mean is it simply parents and their children?
"Blood runs thicker than water"
Or is it allowed to include those people
who are close to us
closer than our own sons and daughters
What makes a group a family?
Is it simply the fact
they descended from a common ancestor?
Is it the aroma
of those common foods that draw us together?
Daddy's fried fish or lit grill full of steak
Mama's banana pudding or from scratch coconut cake
didn't just feed us
they healed us, blessed us,
held us and beckoned many to come greet us
and be welcomed into the fellowship family

Family has been defined
as a group who for a period of time
are confined
together in one place
whose beliefs are one
but our lives that definition have already undone
for we have crossed the globe
separated due to jobs, illness or in search of our goals
and now
come back to where it all began
despite our busy lives
and our personal plans
despite financial challenges
and the members we've lost
despite the trials and tribulations
between which we are tossed
We've returned and we're accepted
as though we never left
That's what makes us a family
That's what makes us blessed
Despite our differences
This love makes us one
Looped together with our faith
A family is born
A family

A Wedding Poem
(written for Edison and Kalea)

This is your time,
your moment
Where you begin to define,
what your future will be
Take a moment to take it all in
(amongst family and friends)
the well wishes that abound,
the love that surrounds
this place is for you
You two who have gone from being children
to adults,
Parents do you see the results of the seeds
that you planted blooming at this time?
The hopes, the desires for your children
are becoming realized
as you let go
Edison and Kalea begin a new journey,
their journey in love

Love. All the love acronyms in the world
don't help you to learn
Or adequately prepare
for every step that lies ahead
You must trust, have faith
and move on in God's grace
Marriage is trusting each other
with all that you have, all that you are
and all that you hope to be
Your individual decisions
become your (plural) consequences
Decisions you make may include some mistakes
but together you'll learn and grow
and begin to know
who you are meant to be, essentially

Always see each other as a blessing
Remember what drew you to each other
in the beginning
When asked your opinion
give it in love
When making decisions
remember to listen
with Your ears and Your hearts
and not those of your family or friends
Surround yourselves,
but don't drown yourselves,
with a village of support
Don't allow a well-informed village
to get in between your love
While there may be many of us here
who are older
That doesn't always mean
that we are able to shoulder
(with unbiased wisdom)
the isms of marriage
We have not walked in either of your shoes,
so in the end
it's what the two of you
decide to do
that will matter most
and determine how you move forward
We cannot know
We can hope, we can love, we can pray,
the love you feel now is forever and a day.
This is your time, your moment
Where you begin to define,
what your future will be...
May God continue to bless you both eternally!

HESITANT
TO QUIT

I love the picture on the previous page of Hoyt, one of my two grand pups. If he had jumped up onto the counter, he wouldn't have been able to stay there. The only thing in the microwave was a cup of tea, something he didn't even want. Lastly he doesn't like heights, another reason for him to have given up. I felt this picture really represented a challenge for him and his determination to overcome it.

For a period of time in my life I quit. Quit doing things that brought me joy. Life had presented too many challenges. I'd lost the aunt that gave me my start in music to murder, my father due to a blood clot, my oldest sister in a hit and run, my youngest brother while he was waiting to get on the transplant list and my mother due to complications while she suffered from dementia with psychosis. Add to that, I wanted to give my children what I had been so fortunate to have, A mother and father that were together until death separated them. I was divorced and felt like I had let them down.

Quitting is no longer an option. I have come to value this journey called life. Healing is part of that journey and writing is part of my healing. This last section has poetry and song lyrics that deal with issues I hope to address as I journey on. No more hesitations.

I've Felt

I've felt invisible

I've felt so much pain that I've felt like giving up

I've felt downright insane

I've felt hopeless

I've felt denied

I've felt disrespected

I've felt darkness inside

I've felt afraid

I've felt abused

I've felt alone and I've felt used

But despite all these things

I've felt the Love of Jesus in the songs that you sing

What we feel makes us stronger

What we feel gives us sight

What we feel brings us blessings

And turns our darkness to light

A light that will shine much farther

than our hands could reach

It allows us to minister, love, and teach

So I'll continue to praise God

And know His Love is real

Continue this journey

Continue to feel!

I Like To Dream

I like to dream
I like to think there's a world in which I'm going places.
I like to think that the only thing that will hold me back
is when I don't have the true ability
to go forward
Yes, I guess you can see that I like to dream
I can't help but dream
I see a world in which love is colorblind
and true feelings never have to be kept hidden
In my world friendship can be gained from anyone
or anything be he/she human or not
And each friendship is just as valuable as the one before
But I'm still dreaming
DON'T WAKE ME UP
Because there is happiness in my world
People smile real smiles and not the kind that fade
before your back is turned
DON'T TOUCH ME!
LET ME SLEEP!
For within my dream world, I'm allowed to be me!
I feel like I'm a page hidden away in a coloring book
So that a child has yet to find me
and decide my fate.
Here I am free to do anything and everything
With no mind as to ability
And love?
Somebody loves me
Loves me
Loves me

I Am Not A Joke (♪lyrics)

Won't you look inside of me
and meet my tenant Mr. Laugh?
He's lived here for years rent free
to save my heart when pain does pass
Well tonight's my night
and so my song begins
The audience relaxes
their faces turn to smiles
My heart is beating quickly
when the sound of laughter reaches my ears
and my heart dies

I yell loud for all to hear that I am not a joke
But the laughter starts up once again
my knock goes unanswered
"Cause Mr. Laugh, isn't in

One must not give up I've heard
a thousand times before
So once again I sit on stage
and my song begins
Well, I'm almost to the last refrain
when tears swell to my eyes
I think I hear them laughing
I stop
the laughter dies

With all their eyes upon me
I yell loud and clear
I am not a joke

The laughter starts up once again
I reach inside for my friend
But Mr. Laugh still isn't in

Life they say is meant to be lived
and love is meant to be shared
Don't be afraid to be who you are
and show the world that you are here
So once again I sit on stage
once again guitar in hand
I put my fingers on the strings
and pause
for a moment
before I begin
This time my song begins
and for the first time it ends
I let out a joyous shout
and look inside for Mr. Laugh
Mr. Laugh my valued friend
But Mr. Laugh
still isn't in
You know
I
laughed anyway

Maybes Won't Save Me (♪lyrics)

Maybe you care while you stare
and in silence move away
Maybe you say on another day,
a helping hand I'll stretch his way
But maybes, won't save me
maybes are too late
To ease the pain I'm feeling today

Maybe you see what they do to me
and don't think of how it feels
Maybe you know of somewhere I could go
and in time begin to heal
But maybes, won't save me
maybes are too late
To ease the pain I'm feeling today.

I can't see past this minute
I can't think of another day
I don't think anyone will mourn me
Why would they?
'Cause all eyes were upon me
Time and time again
as I took the hits
the words,
the licks
tucked my heart in
and prayed that it would end

Maybe my tears, hide your fears
and wash your pain away
Maybe you've been hurt, this is how you've learned
to ease your own pain
But maybes, won't save me
maybes are too late
To ease the pain I'm feeling today
Maybes, won't save me
maybes are too late

To ease the pain
erase the shame,
take back the hits
the words the licks
tucked in my mind
playing all the time
they're all I feel
they're all that's real

Though maybes, won't save
maybe it's not too late
To save someone
that's near you today...
Though maybes, won't save,
maybe it's not too late
To save someone
that's near you today...

A Flame That Never Dies (♪lyrics)
(written in response to Sandy Hook)

With each story

through our sadness there is glory

for the courage shown in those who gave their lives

Then we come together

regardless of the weather

and stand as one as we sadly realize

That it's time to light the candles

To gather at the cross

It's time to let our love

Ease the pain of the loss

And it's time to call a long lost loved one

To make up with a friend

It's time to light the candles again

Light the candles again

Why does it take tragedy

for the world to show peace

for our hands and hearts to see that we're the same?

Why does one have to die

for us to open up our eyes

and see all there stands for us to gain

If we do more than light the candles

And gather at the cross

Hope and pray our love

Will ease the pain of the loss

If we do more than call a long lost loved one

Or make up with a friend

We'll light a flame that never has to end

A flame that never ends

We can make a lasting difference

with a flame that's lit inside

We can heal the walking wounded

by admitting they're alive

We can change the world forever

if we don't forget the pain

That brought us to this moment

lives lost won't be LOST in vain.....

With each story

through our sadness there is glory

for the courage shown in those who gave their lives

Let's light a flame that never dies

Let's light a flame that never dies

A   flame that never dies

IT'S TIME FOR CHANGE (♪lyrics)

What does it take to believe
that I should receive your freedom?
How many more have to die
justice pushed aside, for freedom?
While we fight to survive
try to abide
too tired to cry
tears set aside
for the next time
Innocence dies in someone's eyes...

it's time for change
It's time for prayer
We can't continue to say
There's no problem here
It's time to unite
It's time to make wrongs right
It's time for change, It's time

How can I get one to see
the you that's in me, clearly?
How do we move from this place
without focus on race to unity
Daily we fight to survive,
try to abide
too tired to cry
tears set aside
for the next time....
Innocence dies... in someone's eyes...

it's time for change
It's time for prayer
We can't continue to say
There's no problem here
It's time to unite
It's time to make wrongs right
It's time for change...
it's time

(rap by Kyle)
Shots are flying hope is dying
Cops and sirens mean that you might not survive this
They say noncompliant open fire
Folks are crying
nowadays it's not surprising
The breaking news is breaking you
I swear they tryna make us hate and break in two
We're living in an age where they bring Ks to school
It's really a disgrace let's make some changes soon
Kids dying in the street
won't change laws because of industry
The president talking's like a villain speech
But meek gets locked up just for wheelieing
It's crazy I don't get it won't listen
Want different go get it
Your visions your mission
You're living for different
Purposes
I promise that

All Our Kids (♪lyrics)

It's a table of love
a table of hope
a table of joy
a table of sorrow
It's where we find and renew
the strength we'll need for tomorrow
It's where our tears and our fears
are soothed with a portion of peace
It's where our dreams become goals
our dreams become real

All Our Kids
need a place at the table
a chair to all their own
All Our Kids
need a place at the table
a place within a home
All Our Kids
need a place at the table
to be nourished by a feast
of love
acceptance
encouragement
praise and peace

It's a table of sisters
a table of brothers
with a mom and a dad
It's where we find family
a kind we've never had
It's where our trials and challenges
are served unconditional love
It's where our grief and disappointments
are defeated with a hug

All Our Kids
need a place at the table
a chair to all their own
All Our Kids
need a place at the table
a place within a home
All Our Kids
need a place at the table
to be nourished by a feast
of love
acceptance
encouragement
praise and peace

At the table all our differences
Create a flavor that's unique
After feasting at the table
We rise no longer weak
We rise up full of promise
Full of a strength that's not our own
Knowing we can face tomorrow
Knowing we are not alone

All Our Kids
need a place at the table
a chair to all their own
All Our Kids
need a place at the table
a place within a home
All Our Kids
need a place at the table
to be nourished by a feast
of love
acceptance
encouragement
praise and peace

Heartbeat of Peace (♪lyrics)

There's so much more to life than fighting

Trying to prove whose wrong or right

Dwelling on what could have been

as we wrestle through the night

There's so much more

in life to focus on

As we take our next steps

Let's be grateful for

each day we live

Grateful for each breath...

Tomorrow's not promised

There's no guarantee

Of what lies before us

What it will be

Stop fighting and listen

To your own heartbeat

Close your eyes

so you can see

Close your eyes

feel the heartbeat of peace

With our eyes closed

there's no colors

With our eyes closed

there's a change

We begin to hear more clearly

Realize we bleed the same

With our eyes closed

peace overflows

wars within us cease

Standing still

freedom becomes real,

Along with unity

Tomorrow's not promised

There's no guarantee

Of what lies before us

What it will be

Stop fighting and listen

To your own heartbeat

Close your eyes

so you can see

Close your eyes

feel the heartbeat of peace

the heartbeat of peace

Drowning

Drowning inside my tears
Pushed down by my fears
of both failure and success
Though
I'm more than blessed
and overdue
to pursue
the purpose You planted in me
my true destiny
that I peek at
wave to
run around
push down
take two steps toward
then
run back through the door
of retreat
and take a seat
in what I know
what has been
content
to just exist
but not really live
exhausted
by the cost
of running from the tears
that stream down my face
the tears that trace
the outline
that defines
what

could've
should've
would've
happened if
I had
listened instead of drifted
tried instead of cried
stood up instead of given up
spoken up instead of shut up
believed I would receive
your guidance and love
if I had just trusted
in You

I'm here
drowning in my tears
praying it's not too late
to take my true place
in You and your word
kicking doubt to the curb
ready to swim...

Life is Challenging

Life is challenging
As a single woman
with desire and passion
Choosing friends
who'd believe and support my dreams
without laughing
Learning to love
without completely losing myself
Learning to hurt without giving up
and saying NO ONE ELSE
will ever get close enough to hurt me again
Without deciding to live,
life minus friends,
Just acquaintances,
faces with names
easy to remember,
quickly unclaimed

Life, as a woman, is challenging
As a married woman...
it's the balancing
between husband's feelings and your own
To work or not to work and your home
friends and your family
agreeing on priorities
thinking "I thought I was grown"
(as you're both going through evolutions of your own)
sometimes losing sight of yourself

seeing life from a distance,
like a doll on a shelf
(and that's with or without kids!)

Life, as a woman, is challenging
As a divorced woman with young kids on your own
Keeping them clean, feeling loved and safe from harm
while still struggling just to eat,
Keep roof overhead,
not end up on the street
As they grow it's their education,
Encouraging them to find their passion
(while allowing them room to make decisions)
Forcing them to grow up,
while not turning a deaf ear
to the obstacles of everyday life
looming near

Life is challenging
as a woman
who sought love and lost,
who's divorced
who sought the perfect family
and fell short
Who was sure of herself one moment
and damaged the next

Who's lost focus
and although remains blessed
has dreams lacking direction,
divorced from their goals
constantly rearranging,
frantically searching her soul
for the next steps she should take
towards what's worth it and what's not
Trying to erase the ink of failure
that just doesn't stop

Life as a woman is challenging
And you ask, am I my sister's keeper?
while I'm struggling with life?
Yes,
I'm still standing
due to my sisters in Christ
Yes, through my testimony,
Yes, through my walk
Yes, through my giving '
cause it's more than just talk
Yes, through my love
Yes, through my song
Yes, through my tears
when words can't right the wrongs

I am my sister's keeper,
through all trials and tests
On my journey towards Christ,
through my sisters I've been kept

To the Left, Right Left

Lord
Sometimes
I am so concerned with disappointing you
or not moving in the manner
you would want me to
that I stand paralyzed
downright traumatized

To the left,
to the left,
to the left, right, left
I hear
but I'm afraid to step
lest
my feet fall on a path
that leads to a trap
and to less than you would have me
to be

So, I sit down
trusting the chair
to be aware
of my weight
and how much it can take
Eyes look
to the left,
to the left,
to the left, right, left

And finally, its safe
to git up

I'm Here!

I'm here! I am here!
Do you see me?
I stand boldly before you.
For I am unafraid.
Despite all of the negatives society may have imposed upon me,
(racism,
bondage,
the struggle for an education),.
I'm here!
I am here and I am not going anywhere.
I'm black.
I'm proud.
I'm free
and I am me.
Ready to live,
ready to take advantage of every opportunity that meets me.
Huh! Nothing or no one can take away what I feel right now!
Right here!
Power! It's within me.
It's jumping screaming
going in all directions.
I am here!
Watch Me!
Watch Me!
There is no other like me.
I'm strong.
I'm dependable.
I am a proud African American woman.
And I
I am here to stay
here to stay.
Don't you get in my way!

The Time Has Come

The time has come

that I thought I could run from

face to face

I stand now in this place

with my own reflection

no longer suffering

rejection

of who I am destined to be

accepting my destiny

move

groove

dance

breathe

the old you (you were carrying)

finally must leave

shed your old skin

allow it to drift

as you start to grow

change and shift

closer to the dream

closer it seems

to that which is mine to take

the time has come

Retiring

You've been on a journey
of learning
while earning a living
but giving so much more in return

A journey of growing
while facing
challenging
risk taking
knowing inside which path was yours

A journey of changes and stages
contemplating and rearranging
to best serve others
while you steadfastly endured

Now, it's time
time to say goodbye and hello
simultaneously
for tears of sadness and joy to rain
while mingling through fond recollections
and the creation of new memories

Pressing forward
And trusting the path
you put your feet on.
Enjoy
knowing the blessing you've been
to so many like me

Trippin' At The White House

The sun's glorious rays dance lightly on my feet
As they glide forward
With no special rhythm
No steady beat...
I'm trippin' at the White House
Silently
My body slices through a wintry breeze
For a moment
The sounds around me
Cease
I'm still moving...
But can't feel
Anything
Weightless
Body moving forward
Mind traveling back
To people I love
No longer here
sitting in the tears
at the base of my eyes
Here am I
Trippin'
at the White House
Father served in World War II
My mother lived through the rationing of shoes
And as my feet hit the cobblestone
In shoes I borrowed... not my own
Huh... ain't this something?
I'm not alone
Just trippin' at the White House
With each step forward
I take two back
in my mind
through to the times
when I felt so sad

who am I
to walk this path
I'm trippin' at the White House
This honor belongs to my father and mother
and encourages every sister and brother
to hold on
for another day
for those things that are standing in your way
won't be there forever
work through the storms of the times
that aren't only on the outside
but the inside of our minds
for nothing is impossible
yes we can
words
of the president
who has set aside times such as these
for the people to realize
how it feels to be free
and trippin'
at the white house
The color of the sky can't match
the glow of the sun that's shining in me
the ground beneath feels smooth
as I glide
inside
without trippn' into the White House
I feel blessed

In 2014 my students performed at a tea hosted by Mrs. Obama and
Dr. Biden at the White House.

This World Is Mine

This world is mine
mine to take,
Mine to mold and shake and bake

This world is mine and don't be mistaken
and think that I'll pass through this world without takin'
everything I want and need to succeed
for I know that it's there and waiting for me

How do I know this?
Well I thought you'd never ask
I know 'cause I've learned from the women in my past

Women like Harriet Tubman,
known for the aid she gave
as "Moses" to many, many a freed slave

Or Rosa Parks, who refused to give up her seat
on a bus in 1955 so that I might be free
Free to sit anywhere, and any time that I choose
and thanks to Mary McLeod Bethune, that includes school
For with a dollar-fifty and tons of knowledge
she started a school that is now a famous college

This world is mine,
come,. take a look
It's mine thanks to women like Gwendolyn Brooks
She was the first black poet to win the Pulitzer prize
and one of the many to open my eyes
to all that this great big ole world has to give
so now it's up to me and how I choose to live

Shall I be a neurosurgeon like Dr. Cannady?
Or follow in Unita Blackwell's shoes
and be a mayor in Mississippi?
Shall I be an actress
on television, screen and stage
and like Cicely Tyson,
carefully choose the roles I'll play?

To sing at the Metropolitan House of Opera, might be nice
and win a 42-minute standing ovation, like Leontyne Price

Oh the choices are endless,
if I make good use of my time
For as I told you before,
this world is mine.

This world is mine
mine to take,
Mine to mold
and shake and bake
This world is mine
and don't be mistaken
and think that I'll pass through this world without takin'
Everything I want and need to succeed
For I know that it's there and waiting for me
I'm an African American woman
with a rich history

Recording in progress
If you would like to be notified when an audio recording of this
book is available, send an email to:

graham.sheena2@gmail.com